The Love That Keeps Us Sane

Living the Little Way of St. Thérèse of Lisieux

Marc Foley, O.C.D.

Paulist Press
New York/Mahwah, NJ

The Publisher gratefully acknowledges use of the following: Excerpt from "Burnt Norton" in *Four Quartets*, copyright © 1936 by T. S. Eliot and renewed 1964 by T. S. Eliot, reprinted by permission of Harcourt, Inc. Excerpt from "East Coker" in *Four Quartets*, copyright © 1940 by T. S. Eliot and renewed 1968 by Esme Valerie Eliot, reprinted by permission of Harcourt, Inc. Excerpt from "The Dry Salvages" in *Four Quartets*, copyright © 1941 by T. S. Eliot and renewed 1969 by Esme Valerie Eliot, reprinted by permission of Harcourt, Inc. Page 105 from *Selected Poems of Rainer Maria Rilke*, edited and translated by Robert Bly, copyright © 1981 by Robert Bly. Reprinted by permission of HarperCollins Publishers, Inc. Canto 1, p. 3 from *Dante's Inferno: Translations by Twenty Contemporary Poets*, edited by Daniel Halpern, copyright © 1993 by Ecco Press. Preface copyright © 1993 by Daniel Halpern. Introduction copyright © 1993 by James Merrill. Afterword copyright © 1993 by Giuseppe Mazzotta. Reprinted by permission of HarperCollins Publishers, Inc.

Cover/book design and interior illustrations by Nicholas T. Markell.

Library of Congress Cataloging-in-Publication Data

Foley, Marc, 1949-
    The love that keeps us sane : living the little way of St. Thérèse of Lisieux / by Marc Foley.
        p.   cm. — (IlluminationBook)
    Includes bibliographical references (p.).
    ISBN 0-8091-4002-0
    1. Christian Life—Catholic authors. 2. Thérèse, de Lisieux, Saint, 1873–1897. I. Title. II. IlluminationBooks.

BX2350.2 .F573 2000
248.4'82—dc21

                                                          00-059859

Published by Paulist Press
997 Macarthur Boulevard
Mahwah, New Jersey 07430

www.paulistpress.com

Printed and bound in the
United States of America

Contents

Acknowledgments

Permission has been granted to the author to reprint excerpts from the following books:

Story of a Soul, translated by John Clarke, O.C.D. Copyright © 1975, 1976 by Washington Province of Discalced Carmelite Friars, Inc. ICS Publications, 2131 Lincoln Road NE, Washington, D.C. 20002.

St. Thérèse of Lisieux: Her Last Conversations, translated by John Clarke, O.C.D. Copyright © 1977 by Washington Province of Discalced Carmelite Friars, Inc. ICS Publications, 2131 Lincoln Road NE, Washington, D.C. 20002.

St. Thérèse of Lisieux: General Correspondence, Vol. 1, translated by John Clarke, O.C.D. Copyright © 1982 by Washington Province of Discalced Carmelite Friars, Inc. ICS Publications, 2131 Lincoln Road NE, Washington, D.C. 20002.

St. Thérèse of Lisieux: General Correspondence, Vol. 2, translated by John Clarke, O.C.D. Copyright © 1988 by Washington Province of Discalced Carmelite Friars, Inc.

Dedication

In gratitude to my dear friend Sandra Gettings
whose love, encouragement, and editorial skills
made this book possible.

IlluminationBooks
A Foreword

When this series was launched in 1994, I wrote that Illumination-Books were conceived to "bring to light wonderful ideas, helpful information, and sound spirituality in concise, illustrative, readable, and eminently practical works on topics of current concern."

In keeping with this premise, among the first books were offerings by well-known authors Joyce Rupp *(Little Pieces of Light...Darkness and Personal Growth)* and Basil Pennington *(Lessons from the Monastery That Touch Your Life)*. In addition, there were titles by up-and-coming authors and experts in the fields of spirituality and psychology.

These books covered a wide array of topics: joy, controlling stress and anxiety, personal growth, discernment, caring for others, the mystery of the Trinity, celebrating the woman you are, and facing your own desert experiences.

The continued goal of the series is to provide great ideas, helpful steps, and needed inspiration in small volumes. Each of the books offers a new opportunity for the reader to explore possibilities and embrace practicalities that can be employed in everyday life. Thus, among the new and noteworthy themes for readers to discover are these: how to be more receptive to the love in our lives, simple ways to structure a personal day of recollection, a creative approach to enjoy reading sacred scriptures, and spiritual and psychological methods of facing discouragement.

Like the IlluminationBooks before them, forthcoming volumes are meant to be a source of support—without requiring an inordinate amount of time or prior preparation. To this end, each small work stands on its own. The hope is that the information provided not only will be nourishing in itself but also will encourage further exploration in the area.

When we view the world through spiritual eyes, we appreciate that sound knowledge is really useful only when it can set the stage for *metanoia*, the conversion of our hearts. Each of the IlluminationBooks is designed to contribute in some small but significant way to this process. So, it is with a sense of hope and warm wishes that I offer this particular title and the rest of the series to you.

—*Robert J. Wicks*
General Editor, IlluminationBooks

Introduction

*S*t. *Thérèse once said that if the saints came back to Earth, most of them would not recognize themselves when reading what we have written about them. Thérèse had no use for a sentimental portrayal of the saints. She believed that for us to experience saints as models of virtue, we have to see their real lives and not their imagined lives. How ironic this belief of Thérèse seems when we consider that she became a victim of a twofold sentimentality: the sentimentality of her times, which found expression in her writing, and the sentimentality of the faithful that has been projected upon her. Guy Gaucher comments:*

She fell victim to an excess of sentimental devotion which betrayed her. She was victim also of her own language, which was that of the late nineteenth century and flowed from the religiosity of her age: a handicap to be overcome.[1]

Many people have an emotional reaction when reading Thérèse. They are repulsed by her saccharine style. Her overuse of diminutives, coupled with a recital of her mortifications in the face of the trivial, sounds infantile. However, those who are able to get beyond their initial reaction to her style will discover a spirituality of substance.

In his biography of Thérèse, Barry Ulanov writes, "I have found myself marveling over her realism, marveling all the more as her true words surfaced from under the sea of sentiment in which it has been drowned for so long."[2]

Realism is a word not frequently associated with Thérèse, but those who are able to perceive the unvarnished truth of her real life will find a highly vulnerable, deeply courageous, flesh and blood woman, dealing with the painful realities of life.

Thérèse's writings recount such things as the death of her mother at an early age; her father's being institutionalized in an insane asylum; her night of faith in which she could no longer believe in an afterlife; and her intense physical suffering from tuberculosis that led to her death at the age of twenty-four.

Also, Thérèse's writings deal with the sufferings and annoyances of daily life that arise from living in close quarters with others, what she called the "martyrdom of pinpricks," for Thérèse did not live with angelic creatures who were untouched by the brokenness of this world.

Several of the nuns of Lisieux Carmel were difficult people to live with. There were a few who were emotionally disturbed, one of whom had to be institutionalized. Thérèse said of one of these nuns, "...if I had an infirmity such as hers, and so defective a spirit...I would despair."[3] Thérèse never glossed over the human condition.

There was also a nun toward whom Thérèse had a natural antipathy. "There is in the Community a Sister who has the faculty of displeasing me in everything, in her ways, her words, her character, everything seems *very disagreeable* to me."[4]*

Thérèse admits that her feelings toward this sister were often so intense that she could not even stand being in her presence. "Frequently when I had an occasion to work with this Sister, I used to run away like a deserter whenever my struggles became too violent."[5]

There was also an elderly nun whom Thérèse volunteered to accompany from place to place. At Thérèse's beatification process, this sister was described as "pretty cranky...very odd and sharptempered."[6] Thérèse experienced this firsthand.

Then there was the prioress, Mother Marie de Gonzague. She was a saintly woman but, nevertheless, not an easy person with whom to live. She was very erratic in

*The translator of *Story of a Soul* and *The General Correspondence, Vols. 1 and 2* used in this book italicized words that were underlined by Thérèse in the original text and capitalized words that she wrote in large script because these words were of special significance to her.

her behavior and subject to fits of jealous rage. In a testimony at Thérèse's beatification the following was said:

> Mother Gonzague's unstable and eccentric temperament inflicted a lot of suffering on the nuns. Everything depended upon her latest fancy; anything good never lasted for long, it was only by dint of diplomacy and tact that stability could be achieved even for a few weeks.[7]

This testimony was typical of many other testimonies. Thérèse was subjected to Mother Gonzague's mercurial nature when she was "appointed" novice mistress.

> [Thérèse was] appointed to assist her and substitute for her as the need arose. Because of the prioress's fickleness, Sister Thérèse hadn't a moment's security in this so-called office, which was taken from her and given back again every two weeks or so.... If Sister Thérèse's influence was too strong Mother Prioress was offended and said she had no right to be giving us advice. We novices had to be crafty to avoid conflict, and we had recourse to a thousand stratagems.[8]

Many of us who have ever worked for a boss who was so erratic that what was true one day was not true the next can empathize with Thérèse in this circumstance.

Also, it is important to note that three of the nuns with whom Thérèse lived with were her siblings, Pauline, Marie, and Céline. Even though Thérèse loved them very much, she still had to deal with the interpersonal conflicts that exist among all siblings. To say the least, Lisieux Carmel was not heaven on earth for Thérèse.

Like all of us, she struggled with the human condition and had to find a way to deal with it. Her way was love. She learned to love people as they were, not as she wanted them to be. Her "little way" was her means of holiness, and it was also what kept her sane.

Many books have been written on the "little way" as a means to holiness. This is not one of them. This is about Thérèse's spirituality as a means of preserving sanity in an often insane world. Thérèse's sanity lay in her ability to be deeply involved in life without becoming absorbed by it. She had the genius of knowing how to love others without becoming entangled or enmeshed in their problems. She could deal with the absurdities of daily life without losing her perspective.

Perspective was at the core of Thérèse's sanity. She saw all things in the light of eternity. This vision gave her a sense of proportionality that kept her sane. This book is about the choices that fostered this perspective: knowing what secrets should be kept, knowing how to choose one's battles wisely, not seeking the approval of others, minding one's own business, and letting go of the need to see the fruits of one's labors.

These are the choices that rooted Thérèse's life in God. They kept her sane.

Chapter One
The Secrets That Keep Us Sane

*T*he Soul selects her own Society—
Then—shuts the Door—
To her divine Majority
Present no more—
                    Emily Dickinson

The word *secret*, derived from the Latin *secretum*, carries with it the connotations of separation and discrimination. Secrets are instruments of discernment. They determine where the lines of demarcation between the inner and outer world are drawn. Secrets are walls. They can isolate us or protect us, depending upon the nature of the secret. [1]

Carl Jung wrote that dark secrets are like poison that can drive us insane. Over time they can so infect the psyche that they result in a complete disruption of the inner and outer worlds.[2] Jung gives an example of such a secret in his autobiography.

A woman came into his office out of the need to confess that twenty years before she had murdered a friend out of jealousy.

> She poisoned her best friend because she wanted to marry the the friend's husband. She had thought that if the murder was not discovered, it would not disturb her.... Moral considerations were of no importance to her, she thought.... The consequences? She had, in fact, married the man, but he died soon afterwards, relatively young. During the following years a number of strange things happened. The daughter of this marriage endeavoured to get away from her as soon as she was grown up.... the mother lost all contact with her.
>
> This lady was a passionate horsewoman and owned several riding horses of which she was extremely fond. One day she discovered that the horses were beginning to grow nervous under her. Even her favorite shied and threw her. Finally she had to give up riding. Thereafter she clung to her dogs. She owned an unusually beautiful wolfhound to which she was greatly attached. As chance would have it, this dog was stricken with paralysis.... If someone has committed a crime and is caught, he suffers judicial judgment. If he has done it secretly...the punishment can nevertheless be visited upon him, as our case shows.

As a result of the murder, the woman was plunged into unbearable loneliness. She had even become alienated from animals. And in order to shake off this loneliness, she had to make me share her knowledge.[3]

The dark secrets of our lives can fill us with unbearable pain because they isolate and estrange us from ourselves and the world around us. Like the woman who came into Jung's office, such secrets also compel us to share, in order to unburden ourselves of crushing loneliness.

In our day, we are all too aware of how living with a secret can become a way of life. Most bookstores today have a growing section entitled "Recovery," containing books on alcoholic and dysfunctional families, physical and sexual abuse, shame-based lifestyles, and so on, all of which have the "Don't Tell" rule in common. The fear of exposure that is at the heart of a shameful or guilt-ridden secret can be so strong that our life's goal becomes to conceal it from the world. The secret permeates our consciousness. We are constantly living with the knowledge that we are hiding something. "We dance round in a ring and suppose," writes Robert Frost, "But the Secret sits in the middle and knows."[4] There is much truth in the "Twelve Step" saying, "We are as sick as our secrets." But just as certain secrets make us sick, other secrets can keep us sane.

We have a symbol of this type of secret in Dickens's ghost story *The Holly-Tree*. The protagonist relates the following to a friend.

More than a year before I made the journey...I had lost a very near and dear friend by death. Every night since, at home or away from home, I had dreamed of that friend; sometimes as still living; sometimes as returning from the world of shadows to comfort me; always as beautiful, placid and happy.... It was at a lonely Inn in a wide moorland place, that I halted to pass the night. When I had looked from my bedroom window over the waste of snow on which the moon was shining, I sat down by my fire to write a letter. I had always, until that hour, kept it within my own breast that I dreamed every night of the dear lost one. But in the letter that I wrote I recorded the circumstance, and added that I felt much interested in proving whether the subject of my dream would still be faithful to me, travel tired, and in that remote place. No. I lost the beloved figure of my vision in parting with the secret. My sleep has never looked upon it since, in sixteen years....[5]

Why did the beloved figure vanish? It was depersonalized. It ceased to be a presence the moment it was treated as an object of speculation.

Similarly, whenever we expose an intimate part of ourselves, a quality of self-presence is lost. We can never look upon that part of ourselves in the same way again; our gaze has been altered and infected by the evaluations and judgments of others. It is like sharing with others how deeply we are touched by the beauty of a painting. If the people we are sharing with begin to criticize the quality of the painting, point out to us its flaws or the artist's immature style and the like, we feel demeaned and diminished. For it isn't just the painting that is being judged, but an intimate part of ourselves. And those things that are most intimate about ourselves are also the most vulnerable to the criticisms of others.

From that point on, we can never look at our beloved painting in the same way again, for our inner vision has been infected by the judgments of others. Even when we are alone with our painting, we are not alone. Because we have internalized the judgments of others, we feel that people are looking at the painting with us. As a result, we cannot allow ourselves to be touched by the beauty of the painting as we were previously, because we cannot risk being shamed again. In short, we cannot be present to it. A presence has vanished. In a similar way, Thérèse experienced, at a tender age, the damage that is done when we expose a secret grace to the curiosity of others.

When Thérèse was ten, she suffered from a mysterious illness that left her bedridden for several weeks. One day when she was crying frantically, her sister Marie knelt down before a statue of Mary and prayed for Thérèse to be cured. Thérèse fixed her eyes on the statue, and her crying ceased as a great peace descended upon her.

> All of a sudden the Blessed Virgin appeared *beautiful* to me,...her face was suffused with an ineffable benevolence and tenderness, but what penetrated to the very depths of my soul was the *"ravishing smile of the Blessed Virgin."* ...Ah! I thought, the Blessed Virgin smiled at me, how

happy I am, but never will I tell anyone for my *happiness would then disappear.*[6]

However, Marie coaxed Thérèse to reveal what had happened and asked permission to tell the nuns at Lisieux Carmel. Thérèse agreed reluctantly. When Thérèse went to Carmel to give her account of her miracle, she was bombarded with questions that so confused her that she began to doubt her own experience. And just as she had thought, her happiness disappeared.

> I was unable to resist her very tender and pressing questions; astonished at seeing my secret discovered without my having revealed it, I confided it entirely to my dear Marie. Alas! just as I had felt, my happiness was going to disappear and change into bitterness. The memory of the ineffable grace I had received was a real *spiritual trial* for me for the next four years....
>
> Marie, after having heard the simple and sincere recital of "my grace," asked me for permission to tell it at Carmel, and I could not say "no." ...I was questioned [by the nuns] about the grace I had received. They asked me if the Blessed Virgin was carrying the Child Jesus, or if there was much light, etc. All these questions troubled me and caused me much pain, and I was able to say only one thing: "The Blessed Virgin had appeared *very beautiful*, and I had seen her *smile at me*." It was her *countenance alone* that had struck me, and seeing that the Carmelites

had imagined something else entirely (my spiritual trials beginning already with regard to my sickness), I thought I *had lied*. Without any doubt if I had kept my secret I would have kept my happiness.... I was not able to look upon myself without a feeling of *profound horror*.[7]

Thérèse instinctively knew that this grace was for her alone. Even the mediating instrument of the grace, a smile, conveyed this. A smile is something exclusive by its very nature. When we smile, we can look into the eyes of only one person. It is an I-Thou experience. Thérèse's profound horror was the guilt akin to violating a secret given in strictest confidence.

What Thérèse had violated was herself because she had violated the very nature of the secret. When we try to communicate an incommunicable experience, it ceases to be an experience. It is depersonalized. It becomes an event, something that happened in the past. In Thérèse's words, it became a memory of a grace.

St. John of the Cross writes that when a soul has been touched deeply by a grace, to expose it, even to the noise of one's thoughts and reasonings, shatters the inner solitude necessary for a "deep and delicate listening" that is needed for the grace to have its full effect.[8] How much more damage happens when one's secret is exposed to the eyes of an inquisitive world!

This was a painful lesson for Thérèse but one that she never forgot. Speaking of a grace she had received at her first communion, a year after her cure, she wrote the following:

The "beautiful day of days" finally arrived. The *smallest details* of that beautiful day have left unspeakable memories in my soul!... I don't want to enter into detail here. There are certain things that lose their perfume as soon as they are exposed to the air. There are deep *spiritual thoughts* which cannot be expressed in human language without losing their intimate and heavenly meaning; they are similar to *"...the white stone I will give to him who conquers, with a name written on the stone which no one KNOWS except HIM who receives it."*[9]

Thérèse learned that certain secrets are insepa-rable from our deepest identity and our relationship with God. It is not by accident that she uses the symbol of a stone to express this truth. For a stone is an archetypical symbol of the eternal within us. As Marie-Louise von Franz puts it, "...the stone symbolizes what is perhaps the simplest and deepest experience—the experience of something eternal...."[10]

Thérèse discovered that keeping certain secrets keeps us connected to the eternal. It prevents us from becoming dissipated in the world like a perfume exposed to the air. It fosters spiritual self-consciousness. It connects us to our deepest self and to God. As Russell Lockhart observes, "...the deeper purpose of secrecy is not to cover up what the ego wants to hide but to bring the ego into connection with the Self...."[11]

We cannot be truly sane without being connected to our deepest Self and to God. When we share our inner life indiscriminately, something is lost. Experiences of God's grace that we should keep to ourselves need not be explicitly religious. For example, an experience of beauty may so touch us that to recall it in memory can produce the initial impression that it first had upon us. We have an example of this in Stephen King's story, "The Body." One night four teenage boys camped out in the woods. Early the next morning, one of the boys, Chris, woke up early and took a walk. During his walk he encountered a beautiful deer that touched him deeply. There was something about the experience that told Chris that he should keep it to himself.

> It was on the tip of my tongue to tell them about the deer, but I ended up not doing it. That was the one thing I kept to myself. I've never spoken or written of it until just now, today. And I have to tell you that it seems a lesser thing written down, damn near inconsequential. But for me it was the best part of the trip, the cleanest part, and it was a moment I found myself returning to, almost helplessly, when there was trouble in my life—my first day in the bush in Vietnam, and this fellow walked into the clearing where we were with his hand over his nose and when he took his hand away there was no nose there because it had been shot off; the time the doctor told us our youngest son might be hydrocephalic (he turned out just to have an oversized head, thank God); the long crazy weeks before my mother died. I would find my thoughts turning back to that morning, the scuffed suede of her ears, the white flash of her

tail.... The most important things are the hardest to say, because words diminish them.[12]

This passage touches on the nature of those secrets that keep us sane. They are sanctuaries in both senses of the word. They are sacred places that provide refuge. They keep us sane because they ground us in our Holy of Holies and shelter us from the raging storms of life. They keep us centered in our deepest self, where we know that, in spite of the horrors of life, there is a deeper, more benevolent reality at the heart of the universe. For Thérèse, such experiences of beauty kept her sane by maintaining her sense of perspective.

Shortly before Thérèse entered Carmel, she took a train ride through the Alps to Rome. The beauty that she saw was breathtaking. She wrote the following of this experience:

> When I saw all these beauties very profound thoughts came to life in my soul. I seemed to understand already the grandeur of God and the marvels of heaven. The religious life appeared to me *exactly as it is* with its *subjections*, its small sacrifices carried out in the shadows. I understood how easy it is to become all wrapped up in self, forgetting entirely the sublime goal of one's calling. I said to myself: When I am a prisoner in Carmel and trials come my way and I have only a tiny bit of the starry heavens to contemplate, I shall remember what my eyes have seen today. This thought will encourage me and I shall easily forget my own little interests.[13]

Like Chris, King's protagonist, Thérèse returned to a graced moment to keep her sanity, or, perhaps more accurately, the grace of the experience, abiding in memory, drew her like a magnet in times of need. A past grace is never completely past tense. St. John of the Cross says that a past grace, recalled in memory, still retains something of the original experience.

> Though the effect produced by the remembrance of this communication is not as strong as at the time the communication was received, yet, when the communication is recalled, there is a renewal of love and an elevation of the mind to God.... This is consequently a great grace, for those on whom God bestows it possess within themselves a mine of blessings.[14]

Because grace is still operative in memory, we need to exercise caution even in sharing the "past" experiences of our lives; some memories are meant to function as solitary haunts into which we can retreat and find refuge from the world.

As Thérèse grew in wisdom and age, she became more discerning regarding with whom and to what extent she would share her inner life. Obviously, she shared her inner life, or we would not know so much about her. But she did so only with her intimates, and even with them, she was selective about what she shared of her soul.

The soul may be likened to a beautiful garden that contains delicate and precious flowers. In order to protect the flowers, we need to be selective about whom we invite into our garden. In our discernment two extremes should be avoided.

The first is a lack of discrimination concerning with whom we share our life. It is like not having a wall around our garden; anyone can traipse through it at will. It is like casting our pearls before swine. Swine are not evil; they are simply ignorant of the worth of pearls. They trample on them unaware.

In our desire to be accepted or understood, we can expose ourselves to being stepped on. How often have we been hurt by an unthinking comment upon our lives that follows upon self-disclosure? But even if a hurtful remark is not expressed, there is still the danger that we will be diminished by self-disclosure. Like Dickens's protagonist, by the very act of exposing ourselves to curiosity, we risk the danger of being depersonalized.

An example of this danger is the afternoon talk show. When we make an exposé of our intimate life, we vulgarize it in our own eyes. When we make a tabloid out of our intimate and personal secrets, can we ever behold them as precious again?

The other extreme is to have a wall that completely encircles our garden, a wall so high that nothing gets in, not even sunlight. Because of a lack of human warmth and connectedness, our flowers wither in the darkness of loneliness, and we shiver with the cold fear and anxiety of isolation.

As our defensive walls grow, they press in upon us. Fear begins to suffocate us; it strangles us and backs our lives into a corner. And as our life shrinks, the world becomes filled with menacing monsters. Our souls become saturated with a vague apprehensiveness that Karen Horney calls basic anxiety, which is the "feeling of being isolated and helpless in a world conceived as potentially hostile."[15]

In my own life, this apprehensiveness is connected with my work. When I feel that I am falling behind schedule regarding a deadline, I begin to panic. I feel that "something," I know not what, is pursuing me and gaining ground. I'm afraid that if it ever catches up with me, something horrible is going to happen. In fright, I begin to increase the pace of my life by snatching at every available moment for work. To do this I barricade myself against anything that threatens to consume my time. Community members, friends, necessary recreation are all put on hold, and I tell myself the now familiar lie, "When things get back to normal, my life will be different." But it never is. Both extremes, having no wall or a wall that completely encircles our garden, are to be avoided.

To avoid these extremes, we need a wall to protect our garden from harm, but we should have a gate in the wall, and stationed at the gate, a discerning gatekeeper who selects the soul's company with wisdom.

Thérèse knew how precious and fragile are the deep graces that God implants in the secret garden of the soul. The pain caused by revealing her "secret" to the Carmelite nuns was deep, but it came to good, for it impressed upon her a great lesson that became a characteristic stamp of her spirituality. As she matured, the importance of living a "hidden life" became central to her way to God.

Chapter Two
Finding Her Way

"*Your Face is my only Homeland.*"
St. Thérèse

The "hidden life" represents Thérèse's choice to live before the eyes of the world in such a way that she would not draw attention to herself. Keeping secret her choices to do God's will permeated every area of her life. Ida Gorres comments:

> At all costs she did not want to be "interesting"— not mysterious, noteworthy, enigmatic, stimulating. She did not want to attract the curious glances of the others, to seem admirable or "heroic"....

The veil of ordinariness, averageness, common-placeness...was the guardian of all secrets between God and the soul.[1]

Thérèse's donning of the cloak of ordinariness and her refusal to put on the trappings of the "heroic" flew in the face of the spirituality of her times.

The scholar, André Combes, who had access to the archives to Lisieux Carmel, writes the following about the prevailing spirituality of that convent at the time that Thérèse entered.

> The apostolic doctrine of the French Carmel is contained fully in the notion by which a Carmelite nun is put in the place of a sinner, acting as his substitute.... When this plan was taken literally, the fidelity of the nun to her calling was judged according to the intensity of her spiritual and bodily mortifications. Spiritual mortifications not readily admitting to measurement, much insistence was laid upon corporeal austerities.
>
> This was the ideal in favor at the Carmel of Lisieux under the government of Mere Marie de Gonzague. The cross of Iron and the whip of nettles were then held in high honor.[2]

This vision of the Carmelite vocation was a distortion of what St. Teresa of Avila had in mind. Guy Gaucher comments:

> The Spanish foundress [St. Teresa], full of common sense and with her feet on the ground, laid

down a balanced way of life where love must take precedence over all, including the practices of mortification, which are only means. Three centuries later some Carmels had been diverted towards indiscreet ascetical practices, sometimes towards a narrow moralism. The Lisieux Carmel had not escaped these tendencies which the general climate of French Christianity—with its Jansenist learnings—encouraged. The spirit of penance and mortification was in danger of taking precedence over the dynamism of love. More than one Carmelite was terrified of God the Judge.[3]

At first, Thérèse tried some of these indiscreet ascetical practices, but came to the conclusion that not only was she incapable of doing them, but, more significantly, they were not her way to God. Once, after becoming sick as a result of wearing an iron cross with sharp prongs against her bare chest, she told Pauline that these types of mortifications were not a part of God's will for her.

> She told me how she wore her little iron cross for a long time and that it made her sick. She told me, too, that it wasn't God's will for her, nor for us to throw ourselves into great mortifications; this sickness was a proof of it.[4]

So what was God's will for Thérèse? What path should she follow, now that she was convinced that the "Ideal" of the group was not her calling? God gave her the answer.

One day, when Thérèse was depressed over not knowing her particular calling in Carmel, she went to the infirmary to visit a saintly old nun, Mother Geneviève. Because the limit of two visitors was already in the room, Thérèse smiled and began to leave. "Wait my little child," said Mother Geneviève, "I'm going to say just a little word to you.... Serve God with *peace* and *joy*; remember, my child, *Our God is a God of peace*."[5] These words were such a balm to Thérèse's troubled heart that she was convinced that God had revealed the state of her soul to Mother Geneviève.

The following week, Thérèse visited Mother Geneviève. Thérèse asked her what special revelation God had given her. "She assured me she had received *none* at all, and then my admiration was greater still when I saw the degree to which Jesus was living within her and making her act and speak."[6] The simplicity and unpretentiousness of her response so touched Thérèse that she exclaimed, "Ah! that type of sanctity seems the *truest* and the *most holy* to me, and it is the type that I desire because in it one meets with no deceptions."[7]

Authenticity became one of the hallmarks of holiness for Thérèse. What she heard in Mother Geneviève's response that touched her so deeply was what she *hadn't* heard. There was no phony piety, no affectation, no feigned holiness.

"I love only simplicity, I have a horror for pretense."[8] The opposite of simplicity for Thérèse was not complexity but duplicity. For Thérèse, there was nothing more duplicitous than trying to create an artificial aura of sanctity. As Patricia O'Connor comments, "She avoided conventional pious phrases...and recoiled from creating a haze of artificial mystery."[9]

Thérèse felt that hidden snares of pride were contained in spiritualities that overly emphasize extraordinary mortifications. When talking of these mortifications, she once said to Pauline, "We must be very restrained on this point, for often nature is involved in this matter more than anything else."[10] She knew that we can very easily take pride in our penances and then talk about ourselves in such a way so as to create an image of sanctity. As Thérèse put it, "There is so much self-love mingled with spiritual conversations."[11]

One of the greatest dangers in the spiritual life is wanting to be known as holy. Not only does pride damage our souls, it is also a main source of insanity, because it feeds our fear of what other people think of us. Pride gradually transforms us into actors upon a stage who become more and more dependent upon the applause of an audience.

In Dante's *Inferno*, the hypocrites (the word means *actor*) are clothed in huge choir robes made of solid lead, gilded on the outside with gold. The cloaks are so heavy that the hyprocrites can hardly move. What a graphic image of the desperate need to be recognized by others and the bone-weary insanity of trying to keep up appearances![12]

Thérèse dealt with this reality one day when a novice spoke to her of the great fatigue that her work was causing her. Thérèse asked her how she felt when she was paid a compliment for her work. The novice said, "I feel revived." "It sounds like it's not the work that is causing your fatigue," said Thérèse, "but your need to have your work recognized." When the motive of our actions is to gain either the recognition or approval of others, we drain ourselves emotionally.

The "hidden life" counteracted this need for recognition and protected Thérèse from playing before an audience. However, being protected from *playing* before an audience did not protect her from the *criticism* of her audience. Far from being a shield of invisibility that protected her from the critical gaze of the world, living a "hidden life" actually made Thérèse more vulnerable to the misunderstandings and rash judgments of others.

This was because the other nuns looked at her in relationship to the "Ideal of Carmel," which emphasized physical mortifications. Like the ideal of any group, it functioned as the yardstick of comparison. It was the lens through which the nuns judged one another's holiness.

Thérèse did not fare very well under such scrutiny. As she was dying, Thérèse overheard one nun say, "I don't know why they talk so much about sister Thérèse; she doesn't do anything remarkable. We never see her practicing virtue; in fact she could hardly be called even a good religious!"[13] Another nun said, "Sister Thérèse gets no merit for practicing virtue; she has never had to struggle for it."[14] And one nun wondered what the prioress would be able to say about Thérèse in her obituary. "Sr. Thérèse will die soon.... She entered Carmel, lived here and died. There is nothing more that can be said." In the minds of many, Thérèse was a mediocre nun.

In a certain sense, this was one of her goals: not *being* a mediocre nun, but being *thought* of as one. In a letter to Marie she wrote, "Ask that your little daughter always remain a little grain of sand, truly unknown, truly hidden from all eyes, that Jesus alone may be able to see it...."[15] To be a grain of sand is to put on a guise of ordinariness. It is to be anonymous, to choose to appear average. In commenting on this passage of Thérèse, Conrad De Meester writes:

> She had frequently spoken about the sky, and now the symbolism of the sand was unveiled. Sand is an anonymous mass of small grains, all the same and almost invisible. The grain of sand is the symbol of poverty and littleness of what does not attract attention.[16]

Thérèse's choice to seem average in the eyes of the world involved a deep transformation of the ego and the purification and redemption of the quest for immortality. There is something in us that says that not to be known or not to be seen means not to exist. As one poet put it, "The smile's one-syllable sign says you're seen so you know you're there."[17]

The prize of fame is visibility. It promises to confer existence upon us by rescuing us from the anonymous mass of undifferentiated humanity. It assuages our fear of annihilation by the promise of immortality.

Let us explore for a moment both the psychological and spiritual dimensions of what is involved in the experience of being visible, being "looked at." In doing so we will come to a deeper understanding of what is at stake in living a "hidden life." Let us begin with an exercise of the imagination.

Picture yourself about to give a talk before a group of colleagues. You are prepared but feel a little nervous. You do not know how the group will respond to your material. Five minutes into the talk, you feel yourself calm down, because you notice that the group is interested in what you are saying. Some are nodding their heads in agreement, and a few are even taking notes. However, a few minutes into your talk you notice a change taking place.

There is a restlessness in the audience. You notice that some people are yawning, and others are looking at their watches. There is even a couple in the back of the room snickering to one another. You begin to feel nervous. This affects your concentration. You lose your place and begin to stumble over your words. You're finding it difficult to breathe. You're beginning to panic. You hear a nervousness in your speech, which increases your fear, because you know that your audience is picking up on your anxiety. You're afraid that you are going to fall apart in front of everyone.[18]

This vignette says something very basic about human nature; namely, when we believe that we are being looked at with love, acceptance, understanding, and approval, we feel secure and connected. When we feel that people are looking at us with disapproval, anger, or criticism, we feel afraid and even terrified. The need to be looked at with acceptance and the fear of being looked at with disapproval, or not being looked at at all, are two of the most powerful forces in our lives. Why? Sigmund Freud offers an explanation from a psychological perspective.

Freud said that an all-permeating part of our self-consciousness is what he called in German the Über-Ich, which literally means the over-I (superego). The image contained in the Über-Ich is that someone is looking down upon us.[19]

If we examine the experience of our emotions such as shame and fear, we will discover that we feel that they are experiences of being "looked at." Shame, for example, is the experience of feeling exposed to the gaze of others. And do not most of our fears come down to "What will other people think of us?" There always seems to be an "other" standing in back of us looking over our shoulder.

Freud believed that this "other" is the internalization of the values, ideals, and mores of our parents and other authority figures that we have incorporated into our personality. Simply put, we tend to look down upon ourselves as our parents looked down upon us. How we gaze or glare at ourselves is a reflection of what we saw in our parents' eyes as we were growing up.

An archetypal story of this internalization process is *The Ugly Duckling* by Hans Christian Andersen. The story begins with the egg of a swan being hatched by a duck in a barnyard. Because it appeared different from the other ducklings, it is looked down upon as ugly.

> The poor duckling was chased and mistreated by everyone…. Even his mother said, "I wish you were far away." …At last, the duckling ran away. It flew over the tops of the bushes, frightening all the little birds so that they flew up into the air. "They, too, think I am ugly," thought the duckling.[20]

Outer evaluation became inner evaluation, but at the end of the story, there is healing.

One day, the ugly duckling caught sight of some beautiful swans and felt an uncanny attraction. "He did not know the name of those birds...yet he felt that he loved them as he had never loved any other creatures."[21] However, because he believed himself to be so ugly, he feared that if he approached them, they would peck him to death. But there was something stronger than fear in him—"a strange longing" that he recognized in their call to one another.

At the end of the story, the duckling approached the swans, expecting to be killed. But to his surprise, they encircled and caressed him. When the duckling opened his eyes, he saw his true image in the water, that of a beautiful swan.

The story of the ugly duckling and Freud's concept of the Über-Ich intimate a deep spiritual truth of our nature, namely, that we can only see ourselves in the eyes of another. As creatures made in the image and likeness of God, this ultimately means that we will find our true identity only in the face of God who mirrors back to us our deepest self.

Dante expressed this primal truth of our existence when he put into the mouth of his beloved Beatrice the reason why God created us.

> Not to increase His good, which cannot be,
> But that His splendour, shining back, might say:
> *Behold, I am,* in His Eternity.[22]

We become fully self-conscious only when we see the "I amness" of ourselves reflected back to us in the face of God. This is why Thérèse cries out to God, "Your Face is my only Homeland."

The "hidden life" is about seeking where our deepest identity and the true source of immortality can be found, in the face of God alone. Thérèse wanted to become like a little grain of sand, hidden from all eyes for a reason: "so that Jesus alone may be able to see it." She sought her true reflection in the face of Jesus alone. Thérèse chose to direct her gaze inward so that the opinion of God alone would matter to her. In doing so, even though she suffered the misunderstandings and rash judgments of others, she freed herself from the exhausting task of trying to win their approval.

Ponder for a moment the numerous ways we spend time and energy in either trying to win the approval of others or protect ourselves from criticism. How often do we try to justify ourselves in the minds of others? How often do we rationalize our behavior, distort the truth, or embellish facts in order to be seen in a positive light? How much of our behavior is posturing or putting on airs in order to impress? How often do we do things merely to enhance our image? How often do we lie or shade the truth to avoid rebuke or to curry favor? How often do we vie to be the center of attention? The list goes on and on and on. How apt is Dante's description of the garb of the hypocrites: "O cloak of everlasting weariness."[23]

Thérèse's means of avoiding this weariness in living the "hidden life" was silence. Let us now consider the various ways that silence preserved her sanity.

Chapter Three
The Sanity of Silence

*T*he Father spoke one Word, which
was his Son, and this Word he
speaks always in eternal silence, and
in silence must it be heard by the soul.

St. John of the Cross

The Swiss philosopher Max Picard wrote the following:

In the moment before man speaks, language still
hovers over the silence it has just left; it hovers between silence and speech. The word is still
uncertain where to turn: whether to return wholly
into the silence and vanish therein or whether to

make a clear break with silence by becoming a sound. Human freedom decides whither the word shall go.[1]

One of the places where we experience the Holy Spirit in our daily lives is in that region of the mind where language hovers, waiting upon choice. There, the Spirit prompts us at two basic moments. First, in the moment between impulse and choice, the Spirit offers us the strength of restraint so that the hateful word, the envious word, the self-seeking word, and so on, will not be born into this world but sink back into the silence. Second, in the moment between inspiration and choice, the Spirit prompts us to convert inner language into sound, the life-giving sounds of kindness, forgiveness, encouragement, or admonition.

Thérèse was attentive to the Spirit's promptings. "He teaches without noise of words. Never have I heard Him speak, but I feel that He is within me, at each moment; He is guiding and inspiring me with what to say and do."[2] Her experience of God's guidance was intuitive. It was a "felt sense." Isn't this often the case with us?

Think of a time when you were just about to speak, but there was an instinctive feeling that prompted you, "Don't say it." Have you ever labeled this experience as God? Thérèse did. She knew when God was asking her to speak and when God was asking her to keep silent.

Speech and silence were the two basic means that Thérèse used in responding to God. We will be focusing on Thérèse's use of silence because it was silence, above all else, that kept her sane. However, before we do so, it must be made clear that her silence was never a substitute for the courage to speak.

A time to speak

One of the stereotypical images of Thérèse is that she was a self-effacing, overly submissive person who never stood up for herself and, out of weakness, allowed others to use her as a doormat. Nothing could be further from the truth. Thérèse never shrunk from telling the truth that needed to be told. She confronted situations that everyone else tiptoed around and did so at great personal risk.

For example, when Thérèse noticed that Sr. Martha had developed an unhealthy attachment to Mother Gonzague, she believed that something needed to be said. After much prayer, Thérèse felt that God was asking her to confront Sr. Martha. When she shared with Pauline what she was about to do, Pauline said, "But you run the risk of having your words repeated and then Reverend Mother won't be able to bear the sight of you and you will be sent away to another convent."[3] Considering Mother Gonzague's unstable temperament, these were not empty words. Thérèse responded, "Yes, I know. But since I'm now sure that it's my duty to speak, I cannot let the possible consequences deter me."[4]

Thérèse risked incurring the wrath of the woman who held her future in her hands, and she did so because she felt God wanted her to speak. After she confronted Sr. Martha, Thérèse said the following to her: "Should Mother Prioress notice that you have been crying and asks you who was responsible, you can, if you wish, tell her everything that I just told you."

Thérèse took sole responsibility for her choice. She did not bind Sr. Martha to secrecy, which could have put Sr. Martha in an awkward position with Mother Gonzague. She was willing to bear the consequences of her action. How many of us would have had the courage to do what Thérèse did?

This incident with Sr. Martha illustrates Thérèse's courage in speaking the truth. She did not mince words out of fear of what other people would think of her. "If I'm not loved, that's just too bad! I tell the whole truth, and if anyone doesn't wish to know the truth, let her not come looking for me."[5]

Thérèse spoke the truth regardless of what people would think of her. In her work with the novices, "She was not afraid to be hurt"; says Pauline, "she corrected fearlessly whatever the cost to herself...she never tried to be popular with them."[6] And when she had to correct a novice, she did not succumb to feelings of false guilt.

> We should never allow kindness to degenerate into weakness. When we have scolded someone with just reason, we must leave the matter there, without allowing ourselves to be touched to the point of tormenting ourselves for having caused pain or at seeing one suffer and cry. To run after the afflicted one to console her does more harm than good. Leaving her to herself forces her to have recourse to God in order to see her faults and humble herself. Otherwise, accustomed to receiving consolation after a merited reprimand, she

will always act, in the same circumstances, like a spoiled child, stamping her feet and crying until her mother comes to dry her tears.[7]

However, giving correction was not an easy task for Thérèse. "I find the Prophet Jonas very excusable when taking to flight rather than announcing the ruin of Niniveh. I would prefer a thousand times to receive reproofs than to give them to others."[8]

In spite of her aversion to giving correction, Thérèse never took refuge in silence when it was her duty to speak. In fact, she was so honest that when any of the nuns needed to hear the truth, they instinctively went to her. Céline comments:

> Though not everybody admitted it, all went to her for guidance at one time or another; she was not soft or easygoing, but people turned to her out of a natural need for the truth. Some of the elder nuns went to her secretly, like Nicodemus, when they needed advice for themselves.[9]

What made the truth that Thérèse spoke so attractive was that it was pure. Like Mother Geneviève's, what the nuns heard in Thérèse's words was what they *didn't* hear. There was never a hidden agenda or ulterior motive lurking behind what she said. Her words were free of the dross of egotism and self-interest. They were without alloy, seven times in the furnace refined. And the crucible in which they were purified was silence.

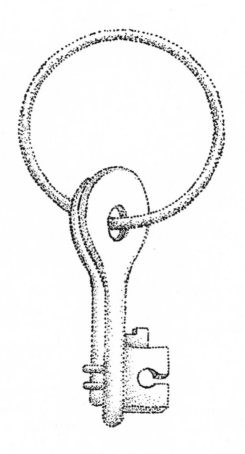

A time to be silent

> Silence is the cross on which we must crucify our ego.
>
> St. Seraphim of Sarov

Thérèse suffered in silence, but always in response to God's will. She never suffered in silence because it was the pious thing to do. Sometimes her silence was an act of charity. At other times, it was an act of humility, and still, at other times, it was an act of mortifying the clamor of her ego. It is this latter motive that we will focus on because it was the one, above all others, that kept her sane.

Choosing battles wisely

> What we choose to fight is so tiny...
> When we win it's with small things,
> and the triumph itself makes us small.[10]

Once when Thérèse was returning some keys to the cell of Mother Gonzague, another nun, believing that Thérèse would awaken the prioress, said that she would return the keys. Thérèse refused. "I was too stubborn to give them to her and to cede *my rights*."[11] An argument ensued that awakened Mother Gonzague. When she opened the door, "The poor Sister whom I had resisted began to deliver a whole discourse, the gist of which was: It's Sister Thérèse of the Child Jesus who made the noise; my God, how disagreeable she is, etc."[12]

Thérèse had a desire to defend herself but walked away without saying a word. Why? Because in the moment,

God had revealed to her that something more important was at stake. "I had a great desire to defend myself. Happily there came a bright idea into my mind, and I told myself that if I began to justify myself I would not be able to retain my peace of soul."[13]

Thérèse hid the truth of what happened because in the inspiration of the moment, it dawned upon her that if she began to justify herself in little squabbles like this, there would be no end to them.

How true this is! We can become so consumed by the petty bickerings and meaningless squabbles of daily life. Where do most of them go? Nowhere! So much of life can be much ado about nothing. Like Thérèse, when we look back over our lives, we often shake our heads and say, "Alas!... I made so much fuss over such little things."[14]

What we often choose to fight is so tiny, and we become small in the process. The more we choose to become absorbed in the trivial battles of daily life, the more petty we become and the more our emotional life becomes fixated on things that don't matter.

When I find myself spending a hundred dollars of emotional energy over a ten-cent issue, I try to remember the wisdom of Thérèse and ask myself the question, "Is it really worth it?" Many times I have won an argument but walked away the loser because my peace of soul was lost in the process. In the wake of so many arguments, our ego may experience the momentary satisfaction of having won, but what have we really gained?

When Céline made her profession, Thérèse made her a coat of arms with this motto on it: "The loser always wins."[15] This motto is applicable to many situations in life. We often win by saying nothing because silence preserves our peace of soul. "What good does it do to defend or explain ourselves. Let the matter drop and say nothing.... O blessed silence that gives so much peace to souls!"[16]

Thérèse learned that to defend or explain herself in certain situations was useless.

> When Mother Geneviève died, Thérèse's relatives and people who worked for the convent sent wreathes. Thérèse arranged them around the coffin. Sister X said to Thérèse, "Ah! You're well able to put the wreathes sent by your relatives in a prominent place, aren't you? And you put those of the poorer families in the background." To this hurtful remark Thérèse said, "Thank you, Sister, you're right. Give me that cross of moss the workers sent, and I'll put it out in front."[17]

Thérèse could have defended herself, but she chose not to. She knew that it wasn't worth it. When someone resents us, as Sister X resented Thérèse, she is not going to listen. To fire back in such circumstances would be futile. Thérèse also noticed that she felt despondent and ill at ease with herself after she didn't control her tongue in such situations.

She labeled these feelings as the temporal punishment due to sin, a sort of psychic residue that lingers in the soul. In short, she lost her peace of soul. Conversely, she noticed that whenever she held her tongue, or recast her words in charity, she experienced peace.[18]

Once, when Sr. St. Stanislaus, the infirmarian, went to vespers, she forgot to close the infirmary door and window. This created a strong draft. When Mother Gonzague went to the infirmary after vespers, she found Thérèse shivering and demanded an explanation. Thérèse later wrote:

> I told Mother Prioress the truth, but while I was speaking, there came to my mind a more charitable way of expressing it than the one I was going to use.... I followed my inspiration, and God rewarded me for it with a great interior peace.[19]

Thérèse told the truth, but in love. However, this was not always easy for her to do. There must have been many times when saying a kind word or refraining from saying a bitter word was a decided effort for her. Let us consider a common situation that Thérèse must have encountered in community life.

Sr. Mary goes to Thérèse because she needs to talk about Sr. Ann. Mary is angry and hurt because of Ann's inconsiderate behavior toward her. But since Thérèse has also borne the brunt of Ann's inconsiderate behavior, she shares many of Mary's feelings. Consequently, it is difficult for Thérèse to listen without becoming angry herself.

> If one tells me about her fights with the Sisters, I am careful not to work myself up against this or that Sister. I must, for example, while listening to her, be able to look out the window and enjoy interiorly the sight of the sky, the trees, etc.[20]

Such situations can quickly degenerate into gripe sessions. To prevent this, Thérèse had to curb her tongue, and at times, probably even had to bite it. She did not deny or repress her feelings. Rather, she distracted herself from her feelings, in order that she would not become embroiled in them. Her approach was sane because it was psychologically and spiritually sound.

Clinical research does not support the popular myth that blowing off steam reduces anger. What it does suggest is that distracting oneself with pleasant activity—what Thérèse did—has a calming effect. Carol Tarvis in her book, *Anger, The Misunderstood Emotion*, writes the following:

> The psychological rationales for ventilating anger do not stand up under experimental scrutiny. The weight of the evidence indicates precisely the opposite: expressing anger makes you angrier, solidifies an angry attitude, and establishes a hostile habit. If you keep quiet about momentary irritations and distract yourself with pleasant activity your fury will simmer down, chances are you will feel better, and feel better faster, than if you let yourself go into a shouting match.[21]

Thérèse often chose to keep quiet in order to keep sane. Living in confined quarters with twenty-four other women, Thérèse could ill afford to become emotionally entangled or allied with certain factions and cliques in her community. She chose her battles wisely.

> ...you should live in the monastery as though no one else were in it. And thus you should never, by word or by thought, meddle in things that happen in the community, nor with individuals in it, desiring not to notice their good or bad qualities.... You should practice this with great fortitude, for you will thereby free yourself from many sins and imperfections and guard the tranquility and quietude of your soul.[22]

Living in the monastery, office, and other places, *as though* no one else were in it is not advocating apathy but cautioning against curiosity. Curiosity is like the itch of poison ivy. The more we scratch, the worse it gets. It increases our distractability and destroys the tranquility and quietude of our souls. It is an inner restlessness that is dying to know the latest gossip or dying to tell a juicy tidbit of news. It is often a symptom of a very corrosive spiritual syndrome that the desert writers of the fourth century called acedia (sloth).

Curiosity is an indication that inner alienation is taking place. St. Bernard wrote:

> And so the first step of pride is curiosity. You can recognize it by these indications. You see a monk of whom you had thought well up to now. Wherever he stands, walks, sits, his eyes begin to wander. His head is lifted. His ears are alert. You can

tell from his *outward* movements that the *inner*
man has changed[23] (italics added).

What has changed is the mind's center of gravity. It is no
longer recollected in God and, therefore, its deepest center.
Consequently, the mind is easily distracted. But this is what
it wants. As exhausting as it is to be fitfully yanked around
from object to object, from fantasy to fantasy, from impulse
to impulse, it is nevertheless less painful than to be with
oneself. To paraphrase the poet Yeats, because we are not
being held by our center, mere anarchy is loosed upon the
mind.

But acedia is not just anarchy of mind, but anarchy
of life. For when a person is no longer centered in his own
life, his life becomes dissipated in the lives of others. Curiosity, gossip, eavesdropping, a voyeuristic bent of mind,
always having one's ears attuned for the latest scandal or
Byzantine intrigue—these are symptoms of vicarious living. Meddling in everyone else's business is a symptom of
not having one's mind on one's own business.

Thérèse minded her own business. This was evi-
denced by Céline's comments: "I noticed that she never
asked for news."[24] "She never asked a question to satisfy her
curiosity...."[25]

These practices of restraint, which traditional spirituality has labeled as "custody of the senses," may sound
archaic to the modern ear; they smack of an outdated spirituality. But if we practice them rightly, we will discover
that they can help keep us sane. Custody of the senses
helps keep us sane because it curbs curiosity and helps heal
the impulsiveness that underlies it. Impulsiveness is a form

of insanity that deprives us of self-determination because it robs our choices of intentionality. In his book *Neurotic Styles*, psychologist David Shapiro writes the following of the experience of impulse:

> It is an experience of having executed a significant action, not a trivial one, without a clear and complete sense of motivation, decision, or sustained wish. It is an experience of an action, in other words, that does not feel completely deliberate or fully intended.[26]

A diminishment of intentionality decreases our self-presence because our choices are no longer experienced as a conscious response to life, but as a knee-jerk reaction to it. Life becomes a disconnected series of events devoid of meaning.

Conversely, custody of the senses is a practice that sustains meaning in life because it is a form of the practice of the presence of God. It brings sanity into our lives because it brings us into God's presence. When we consciously choose to do something for the sake of God, our consciousness of God increases.

Custody of the senses can also have a profound impact upon our human relationships. For what do most human encounters consist of, except speaking and listening! And what if our ears and mouth were under the control of grace?

We see this control in Thérèse. Concerning her work with the novices, she says:

> I refrained from asking questions simply for the sake of satisfying my curiosity.... If a novice is telling me something interesting but goes on to tell me something that bores me, without finishing telling me about the other, I am careful not to remind her of the subject.[27]

Thérèse was vigilant against the natural inclination to veer the conversation back to what sparked her interest. She was on guard not only against giving in to vain curiosity, but also against using someone for psychic stimulation. Instead of asking a question out of curiosity, Thérèse chose to let her novices talk about what was important to them. By attending to the person that God had placed before her, Thérèse attended to God's will. This was minding her own business.

Another aspect of minding one's own business that brought sanity to Thérèse was choosing not to fume over things that were outside of her control. An example of this has to do with the political and religious situation of her day.

In 1880, France passed laws against religious orders. Céline was very upset that many religious communities were submitting to these laws. One day she said to Thérèse, "My entire being rises up in rebellion when I witness such a spirit of cowardice. I would be cut into a thousand pieces rather than belong to any of these communities or to assist them in any way."[28] Thérèse responded:

> We should not be concerned about such matters at all. It is true that I would be of your opinion and act perhaps in the same way had I any responsibility in

the matter. But I have no obligation whatsoever. Moreover, our only duty is to become united to God. Even if we were members of those communities which are being publicly criticized for their defections, we would be greatly at fault in becoming disquieted on that account.[29]

Thérèse's advice to Céline is basic for maintaining sanity. It asks her to differentiate what she can do from what she can't do. What could a cloistered nun in nineteenth-century France do about the political situation except pray and be faithful to her vocation? Put positively, *how* does God want Céline to be responsible regarding the political situation of France? Ruminating about what we *would* do *if* our life were different does nothing except churn us up inside and tempt us to neglect what we are called to do.

St. Teresa of Avila wrote that "sometimes the devil gives us great desires so that we will avoid setting ourselves to the task at hand, serving our Lord in possible things, and instead be content with having desired the impossible."[30]

Being able to focus on the task at hand when the whole world is falling in around us not only can keep us sane, but also may be a sign of deep holiness. The two are often interrelated.

Interviewing Mother Teresa of Calcutta, a reporter once asked her:

> "Isn't it terrible, Sister? Ten thousand refugees are pouring into Calcutta every day from besieged Bangladesh, and there is no food or housing for them." "No," replied Mother Teresa,

"it is wonderful. See he just took food," pointing to the shriveled youngster in her arms who had just taken a spoonful of milk.[31]

We see in Mother Teresa and Thérèse an enigmatic sanity characteristic of sanctity, a sanity that is deeply moved by human suffering, but strangely unperturbed by it. This is a mystery of God's transforming grace.

Dorothy Sayers, commenting on this mystery presented in Dante's *Paradiso*, says that the reason saints are simultaneously concerned and untroubled with the evils of this world is that their emotions "are experienced *pure*, and not bound up with a whole complex of confused personal feelings."[32]

We are often confused about what we feel because our feelings are often fused together. For example, our anger may be twisted fear or contaminated by hate, envy, or a desire for revenge. Because it is not pure, it leaves behind a harmful residue in the soul, what spiritual authors call defilement.

There is an anger that defiles us, but there is also an anger that burns clean. Indignation becomes righteous, says St. Thomas, when it springs from pure love. When the motive is pure, so is the effect. And just as grace purges our anger of impurities, so does it purge love of our confused personal feelings.

Our feelings are often confused because they are not entirely our own. For example, we may have jumped on some politically correct bandwagon out of a need to belong or the fear of rejection. Then, over time, we come to believe that we *should* feel a certain way about things and feel guilty if we don't. Perhaps some of what we have labeled in ourselves as a raised consciousness is actually a contaminated one.

Mother Teresa's consciousness was pure. Her concern for the Bangladesh refugees could not contaminate her joy because it sprang from pure love, untainted by either false guilt or the hand-wringing anxiety that does not trust in God's providence. During the interview, when she was feeding the child she held in her arms, she was not distraught about the tens of thousands of refugees from Bangladesh because she was minding her own business, attending to the task at hand.

Finally, minding one's own business helps preserve our sanity because it eliminates the envy and resentment that come from comparing our lot in life with others.

Céline once noticed that God was asking her "to renounce some legitimate pleasures which other sisters could enjoy in peace."[33] She resented this. Why is God asking *me* to do this thing and not others? It's not fair! She told Thérèse of her complaint. Thérèse responded:

> As for me, I do not concern myself about what God might be asking of others; nor do I assume that I store up greater merit when I am obliged to sacrifice more than other souls in His service. Whatever He asks of me always makes me happy.[34]

Thérèse's attitude is sane because it offers a way out of a dilemma that we encounter on the spiritual path. In the process of conversion, we come to a threshold that, once crossed over, cannot be recrossed without inflicting upon ourselves incredible pain. The deeper divine charity takes root in our hearts, the greater the guilt we feel when we hate or fail to love. The more we say yes to God, the more painful it becomes to say no. Nevertheless, we continue to resist God's call to grow. Consequently, we feel trapped. We can't say no, but we don't want to say yes. We resent being put in this position.

St. John of the Cross speaks of this resentment in *The Dark Night of the Soul*. He says that one of the common signs that God is about to lead a person into a deeper process of transformation and conversion is the temptation to blaspheme God. We can interpret this as the soul's revolt against feeling forced to do something it doesn't want to do.[35]

But the soul's blasphemy is often not aimed directly at God. It is displaced and projected upon those around us. What we resent and envy in people who do things that our conscience forbids us to do, is not that they *do* them, but that they don't feel guilty about their actions. If they were tormented with self-reproach we wouldn't despise them. In short, we resent people whom we perceive that God has not trapped as he has trapped us.

However, God has not trapped us. We have trapped ourselves in resentment because we have chosen not to mind our own business. Minding our own business releases us from the trap of resentment and allows us to live in a sane state of mind.

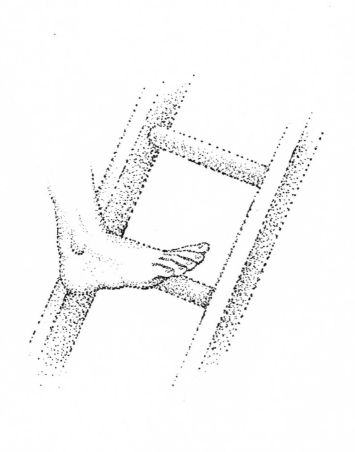

Chapter Four

The Sanity of Loving Freely

*F*or us, there is only the trying. The rest is not our business.

T. S. Eliot

What allowed Thérèse to live in a sane state of mind was not looking beyond her choices for a reward. By focusing on what God was asking her to do, while not being concerned with the results of her actions, she freed herself from much worry and heartache. In this regard, she instructs her sister Céline:

> Be like a child...practice all the virtues and so always lift up your little foot to mount the ladder of holiness, but do not imagine that you will be able to ascend even the first step. No! The good Lord does

not demand more from you than your good will. From the top of the stairs, he looks at you with love. Very soon, won over by your useless efforts, he will come down and take you in his arms. He will carry you up. But if you stop lifting your little foot, he will leave you a long time on the ground.[1]

Continue to lift up your little foot, but do not imagine that your efforts will be successful. Continue to try, but take it for granted that you will fail. That sounds ridiculous! Why would you try something if you believe that you are going to fail before you begin? Isn't this a formula for discouragement and frustration?

Thérèse would say no. In fact, it was her way out of frustration. Frustration is a consequence of failure. Thérèse's image is not an image of frustration because, for her, the *effort* and the *goal* were one and the same. It is only when our goal is *in* the accomplishment of a task, beyond our efforts, that we sow the seeds of frustration. This is because *until* or *if* we are able to get our little foot up over the stair, we will feel that we are failing. But if the goal *is* the trying, then we meet our goal *in* the trying.

What Thérèse is writing about is letting go of our need for results before we begin. Such an inner detachment can help keep us sane. Let's look at an example of this inner detachment from Thérèse's work with her novices. She says to Pauline:

> To the right and to the left, I throw to my little birds the good grain that God places in my hands. And then I let things take their course! I busy myself with

it no more. Sometimes, it's just as though I had thrown nothing; at other times, it does some good. But God tells me: "Give, give always, without being concerned about the results."[2]

To her sister Céline, she says something similar:

Ever since I took over the novitiate, my life has been one of war and struggle.... My only desire has been to please Him; consequently, I have not worried over what others might be thinking or saying about me...nor have I desired that my efforts bear fruit.[3]

By letting go of the desire that her efforts would bear fruit, Thérèse let go of what was not in her control. She knew that she could not make people accept what she said. All she could do was speak the words that she believed God wanted her to say.

Like the sower in the gospel, Thérèse realized that all we can do is sow the seed. The fruitfulness of our actions depends upon the soil on which it lands. If our words fall on deaf ears, shouting louder and wringing our hands in worry will accomplish nothing. Letting go of the need for results in things over which we are powerless is letting go of useless care and worry. T. S. Eliot prayed, "Teach us to care and not to care/teach us to sit still.... Our peace is in your will."[4] Thérèse's peace was the result of differentiating the right kind of care from the wrong kind of care. The right care is in our attentiveness in the doing; the wrong care is in our worry about the outcome. Thérèse kept her sanity because she could be at peace once she had said her piece.

Let's take another example where the doing and the goal were one and the same. Once, Pauline did an act of kindness for another nun and did not receive any thanks for her efforts. She felt hurt and talked to Thérèse about her feelings. Thérèse responded:

> I assure you, I too experience the feelings you are speaking about. However I don't allow myself to be trapped by them, for I expect no reward at all on earth. I do everything for God....[5]

Yes, Thérèse did feel the sting of ingratitude. However, she did not become trapped by her feelings because she didn't bring *expectations* to situations. Since she didn't expect any reward or recognition from others, she was never disappointed when she didn't receive them.

Doing everything for God but expecting no reward on earth isn't doing anything magnanimous. It is simply a formula for sanity, for the more we expect people to appreciate our efforts, the more we make ourselves vulnerable to feeling hurt. Thérèse was not hurt by the ingratitude of others because there were no strings attached to her charity. She gave freely.

What helped her give freely was that she prepared herself mentally in advance, such as anticipating that she would be interrupted in what she was doing. For instance, at the beginning of every free time, the only time she had to do her writing, she would decide to discontinue her writing if a request for her assistance was made. This is an application of St. Paul's advice: "Everyone must give according to what he has *inwardly decided;* not sadly, not grudgingly, for God loves a cheerful giver" (2 Cor 9:7) (italics added).

The reason we often give grudgingly is that we feel that something is being *taken* from us. However, when we have inwardly decided to give, *before* we are asked, the feeling that something is being taken from us disappears because we have already made a choice to *give it away.*

Inwardly deciding about something before it happens is such a sane practice because so much of life is predictable. At home and at work, we rub up against the same people who grate on us in predictable ways. If we know by experience that a certain person will annoy us in a particular way, why can't we prepare ourselves mentally before it happens? This was the advice that Thérèse gave to her novices.

One day Sr. Marie of the Trinity came to Thérèse infuriated about Sr. St. Raphael, who had just cornered her. Sr. St. Raphael was an older sister who, on her free days, loved to engage people in long conversations about spiritual subjects. Most of these "conversations" were nothing more than long tedious monologues about boring subjects. Thérèse told Sr. Marie two things: first, that she should try to be gentle with Sr. St. Raphael; second, "You must soften your heart in advance. After that you will practice patience quite naturally."[6]

To keep one's sanity in community requires a great deal of patience with the foibles, idiosyncrasies, and shortcomings of others. Thérèse knew that if we don't deal with our dislikes, aversions, and animosities, they can consume us. In order not to allow this to happen, Thérèse went out of her way to love people she did not like.

> Not wishing to give in to the natural antipathy I was experiencing (toward Sr. Thérèse of St. Augustine), I told myself that charity must not consist in feelings but in works; then I set myself to doing for this Sister what I would do for the person I loved the most.[7]

In acting against her natural inclination, Thérèse provided a sort of antidote for her feelings. In choosing to incline her will in the opposite direction of her natural bent, Thérèse prevented the insanity of being consumed by her feelings. In choosing to love freely, she freed herself from the insanity that her animosities could inflict upon her. Her choice to love others began by looking for the good in them.

Chapter Five

The Divine Perspective of Charity

hile with an eye made quiet by the power
Of harmony, and the deep power of joy,
We see into the life of things.
William Wordsworth

When Thomas Merton entered the Trappist monastery at Gethsemani, Kentucky, in 1941 he left behind a world that repulsed him. In 1948 he left the monastery for the first time in seven years to accompany a fellow monk to downtown Louisville. Merton expected to see the same sinful world that he had left behind seven years before, but, to his surprise, he discovered something else.

We drove into town with Senator Dawson, a neighbor of the monastery, and all the while I wondered how I would react at meeting once again, face to face, the wicked world. I met the world and I found it no longer so wicked after all. Perhaps the things I had resented about the world when I left it were defects of my own that I had projected upon it. Now on the contrary, I found that everything stirred me with a deep and mute sense of compassion. Perhaps some of the people we saw going about the streets were hard and tough...but I did not stop to observe it because I seemed to have lost an eye for merely exterior detail and to have discovered, instead, a deep sense of respect and love and pity for the souls that such details never fully reveal. I went through the city, realizing for the first time in my life how good are all the people in the world and how much value they have in the sight of God.[1]

This was a moment of revelation for Merton. He did not see God, but what was disclosed to him was how God sees. Merton discovered how people look in the sight of God: *God looked upon everything that he had made and saw that it was very good.* Seeing as God sees is the faith vision, the divine perspective that God calls us to share.

Perspective, derived from the Latin *perspicere,* means "looking through." Grace purifies, transforms, and deifies the lenses of our mind that enable us to "look through" the eyes of God, to see all things from God's perspective.

Thérèse once spoke of this divine perspective by comparing God to the lens of a kaleidoscope.

> This toy...intrigued me, and for a long time I kept wondering just what could produce so delightful a phenomenon. One day a careful examination revealed that the unusual effect was merely the result of a combination of tiny scraps of paper and wool scattered about inside. When on further scrutiny I discovered three looking-glasses inside the tube, the puzzle was solved. And this simple toy became for me the image of a great mystery.... So long as our actions, even the most trivial, remain within love's kaleidoscope, the Blessed Trinity (which the three converging glasses represent) imparts to them a marvelous brightness and beauty.... The eye-piece of the spy-glass symbolizes the good God, who looking from the outside (but through Himself, as it were) into the kaleidoscope finds everything quite beautiful, even our miserable straws of effort and our most insignificant actions.[2]

Grace so transforms our vision that we too see beauty when we look upon what the world deems as straw. St. John of the Cross wrote that souls transformed by grace "see" through the eyes of God.

> And here lies the remarkable delight of this awakening: The soul knows creatures through God and not God through creatures. This amounts to knowing the effects through their cause and not

the cause through its effects...the soul is moved
and awakened from the sleep of natural vision to
supernatural vision.[3]

We cannot acquire this supernatural vision by our
own efforts, for it is the work of divine grace. Nevertheless,
we can choose to cooperate with grace for this transformation to occur.

Grace transformed Merton's vision which freed
him from being fixated on the surface behavior of others,
but this grace involved a choice. "Perhaps some of the people we saw going about the streets were hard and tough...
but I did not stop to observe it."

Merton *saw* the hard and tough exteriors of others,
but he chose not to *focus* on them. This choice freed him
from being fixated on details and, thus, enabled him to see
beyond people's exteriors. This is the tendency of divine
love.

On souls that are perfected in love, St. Teresa of
Avila writes:

> As soon as these persons love, they go beyond the
> bodies and turn their eyes to the soul and look to
> see if there is something to love in the soul. And
> if there isn't anything lovable, but they see some
> beginning and readiness so that if they love this
> soul and dig in this mine they will find gold.[4]

Love has the power to see into the life of things.
Choosing to look *beyond* the irritating behavior of people
in order to perceive the best in them is not some Pollyanna

exercise. It is choosing to focus on that which is most real *in* them. Frederick Faber writes:

> Nothing deepens our mind as much as a habit of charity. Charity does not feed on surfaces. Its instinct is always to go deeper. Roots are its natural food. A man's surfaces are always worse than his real depths. There may be exceptions to this rule; but I believe them to be very rare...charity is the deepest view of life, and the nearest to God's view, and therefore also not merely the truest view, but the only view which is true at all.[5]

Charity grounds us in reality and thus helps to keep us sane. In order to fully understand how much charity and looking for the best in others keeps us sane, we need to first explore the insanity that comes into our lives by focusing on our neighbor's faults and failings.

Reflect for a moment. What has dwelling on your neighbor's faults ever brought into your life? Did it bring peace? Did it bring beauty? Did it bring joy? Didn't it rather warp your vision of life and poison your capacity to see goodness and beauty in life? And when we deprive ourselves of seeing goodness and beauty, do we not deprive ourselves of two of the wellsprings of joy?

The tragedy of what we do to ourselves when we choose to fixate on the faults of others is seen in Jesus' cure of the man with the withered hand.

> On another Sabbath he came to teach in a synagogue where there was a man whose right hand

was withered. The scribes and Pharisees were on the watch to see if he would perform a cure on the Sabbath so that they could find a charge against him. (Luke 6:6–7)

The Greek that is translated "on the watch" (*para-teereo*) may be rendered "lying in wait for." It is an image of a lion, lurking in hiding, waiting for the right moment to pounce upon its prey. This image points to a tragic reality of our lives.

When we are on the lookout for someone to make a mistake, we become blind. The scribes and Pharisees were blind to the beauty of a miracle taking place before their very eyes because all of their sight was lying in wait for Jesus to make a mistake. There was no consciousness left to see anything else. Have you ever waited and hoped for someone to err, so that you could either attack or humiliate him?

A steady diet of fault-finding only makes us disgruntled with life and full of disgust toward others. In Jon Hassler's novel *North of Hope* we have an example of this. In this scene Fr. Frank Healy, who is stationed in his hometown in northern Minnesota, is visiting an old woman he had known in his youth.

> Mrs. Graham, the undertaker's widow, kept Frank in his chair for nearly an hour, pouring out the tedious history of her skirmishes with certain dolts who had sold her a defective car in 1951 and certain other dolts of more recent memory who had sold her a defective television and a defective

health insurance policy. Assenting politely to her accusations and complaints, but giving her only half his attention, Frank contemplated—and was saddened by—the vast difference between this woman and the woman she had been...she seemed to be energized by very little in life except her bitterest memories. Each time Frank tried to change the subject—the weather, the neighbors, the plans for the new water tower—her eyes gazed and she coughed in his face. But at the mention of a person or a streak of luck that had turned against her, her eyes quickened, her voice grew strong, and her coughing went away.... When at last Frank was taking his leave...she said, "You had an Indian funeral last month."

"Yes, a man named Upland."

"My husband buried too many Indians."

"Yes, they die untimely deaths out there."

"I don't mean that. I mean he buried more Indians than he got paid for. I told him not to bury Indians, but he'd always go ahead and do it. He'd always say it's racial prejudice to turn away deadbeats.... I'll bet you weren't given a nickel by the Upland people."

"I was given fish and wild rice."

"I'll bet the rice was seconds. All crumbs."

"We'd have to ask Mrs. Tatzig. It tasted good."

"And the fish was pike, I suppose."

"Yes."

"I hate pike."[6]

What a frightening prospect that over a lifetime we can become a person who reads the worst into every action and feeds upon one's bitterest memories.

Thérèse knew that love prevents this madness because it sweetens our memory. She learned this early on in religious life. As a novice, she volunteered to assist Sr. St. Pierre, an elderly nun, described in Thérèse's beatification process as "pretty cranky…[and] very odd and sharptempered," each evening from the choir to the refectory.

> Each evening when I saw Sister St. Pierre shake her hour-glass I knew this meant: Let's go! It is incredible how difficult it was for me to get up, especially at the beginning; however, I did it immediately, and then a ritual was set in motion. I had to remove and carry her little bench in a certain way, above all I was not to hurry, and then the walk took place. It was a question of following the poor invalid by holding her cincture; I did this with as much gentleness as possible. But if by mistake she took a false step, immediately it appeared to her that I was holding her incorrectly and that she was about to fall. "Ah! God! You are going too fast; I'm going to break something." If I tried to go more slowly: "Well, come on! I don't feel your hand; you've let me go and I'm going to fall! Ah! I was right when I said you were too young to help me."
>
> Finally, we reached the refectory without mishap; and here other difficulties arose. I had to seat Sister St. Pierre and I had to act skillfully in order not to hurt her; then I had to turn back her

sleeves (again in a certain way), and afterwards I was free to leave. With her poor crippled hands she was trying to manage with her bread as well as she could. I soon noticed this, and, each evening, I did not leave her until after I had rendered her this little service.[7]

Years later Thérèse wrote of the fruit of this act of charity:

> Dear Mother, perhaps you are surprised that I write about this little act of charity, performed so long ago. Ah! if I have done so, it is because I feel I must sing of the Lord's mercies because of it. He deigned to leave its memory with me as a perfume which helps me in the practice of charity. I recall at times certain details which are like a springtime breeze for my soul.[8]

Every act of charity deposits joy in the memory because love is of God. And when charity reaches such a depth that it unites us to God, it radically alters the whole inner atmosphere of the soul because the memory, says St. John of the Cross is "changed into presentiments of eternal glory."[9] The soul begins to see all things *sub specie aeternitatis*, in the light of eternity.

Conversely, Thérèse knew that when we are critical of others and don't make the effort to see others in the light of charity, we deprive ourselves of happiness. "It is they [your critics] that are really the losers," Thérèse once said to Céline, "[for] is anything sweeter than the inward joy that comes from thinking well of others!"[10]

Being able to think and see in charity is a costly grace, for it is the fruit of *acting* in charity toward those who trigger either our most unyielding animosities or strongest aversions. Thérèse's charity was tested in these areas in the last year of her life, a time when she was dying of tuberculosis and going through her dark night of faith.

From March 1896 to May 1897, Thérèse volunteered to work in the linen room with Sr. Marie of St. Joseph, a nun with a depressive personality, who had such black moods and violent mood swings that no one was willing to work with her. When Thérèse offered to work with her, it was a fully conscious choice, since Thérèse was very aware of the depth of Sr. Marie's illness. Thérèse once said of her: "She is like an old clock that has to be re-wound every quarter of an hour."[11] Even for Thérèse, Sr. Marie was a difficult person to love. In June 1897, a month after she stopped working with Sr. Marie, Thérèse wrote:

> This year, dear Mother, God has given me the grace to understand what charity is; I understood it before, it is true, but in an imperfect way. I had not fathomed the meaning of these words of Jesus: "The second commandment is LIKE the first: You shall love your neighbor as yourself...." Dear Mother, when meditating upon these words of Jesus, I understood how imperfect was my love for the Sisters.... Ah! I understand now that charity consists in bearing the faults of others, in not being surprised at their weakness, in being edified

by the smallest acts of virtue we see them practice. But I understood above all that charity must not remain hidden in the bottom of one's heart. Jesus has said: "No one lights a lamp and puts it under a bushel basket, but upon the lamp-stand, so as to give light to ALL in the house." It seems to me that this lamp represents charity which must enlighten and rejoice not only those who are dearest to us but ALL who are in the house without distinction.[12]

These words indicate not only what charity cost Thérèse, but also intimate the fruit she received from it. Because she was willing to bear the presence of Sr. Marie, Thérèse was not shocked by her behavior because she was able to see how much Sr. Marie struggled with herself. Thus, she was able to see acts of virtue in Sr. Marie that everyone else was blind to. This fostered a deep sense of compassion in Thérèse. Once, when Pauline asked Thérèse how she could bear working with Sr. Marie, Thérèse responded:

> I assure you that I have the greatest compassion for Sister X. If you knew her as well as I do, you would see that she is not responsible for all of the things that seem so awful to us. I remind myself that if I had an infirmity such as hers, and so defective a spirit, I would not do any better than she does, and then I would despair; she suffers terribly from her own shortcomings.[13]

If you *knew* her you would *see* she is not responsible for the things that *seem* so awful to us. Thérèse was

not trying to exonerate Sr. Marie to Pauline, but she was disclosing to her the insanity from which charity releases us.

The warmth of charity softens our mental rigidity in which our vision has become frozen in judgmentalness and allows us to see the beauty that is before us.

There is a common figure-ground drawing that when looked at one way reveals the face of an old hag, but if we are able to shift our focus, we see the face of a beautiful woman. A judgmental mind cannot make such a shift. It is frozen. It is locked into seeing things in only one way. Consequently, it is blind to the beauty before its eyes.

Graham Greene wrote in his autobiography that he was repulsed by the appearance of a priest he knew; Greene described him as a fat, converted actor. However, over time, Greene realized that his first impressions were totally false and that he was facing the challenge of an inexplicable goodness. Grace unlocked Greene's vision. It allowed him to see beyond his first impressions and disclosed to him the goodness that stood before him.

When we are locked into seeing people through the eyes of our preconceptions, prejudices, and reactions, we lock out of our lives experiences of beauty and goodness. In doing so, we deprive ourselves of these two wellsprings of happiness in life.

"How sweet is the way of *love*," writes Thérèse; "it leaves nothing but a humble and profound peace in the depths of the heart."[14] Love helps to keep us sane because it discloses to us the beauty and goodness of God that permeates this world, for when we see through the eyes of God we are able to see into the life of things.

Chapter Six

An Attended Life,
an Authentic Life

The point of intersection of the timeless
With time is an occupation of the
saint—
No occupation either, but something given
And taken in a lifetime's death in love,
Ardour and selflessness and self surrender.
For most of us, there is only the unattended
Moment, the moment in and out of time,
The distraction fit, lost in a shaft of sunlight…
The hint half guessed, the gift half understood, is
Incarnation.
Here the impossible union
Of spheres of existence is actual.

T. S. Eliot

Perhaps the greatest insanity of life is that we never awaken to the reason we were born. At the beginning of *The Divine Comedy* Dante finds himself in a dark wood, and he doesn't know how he got there. He awakens to the shocking realization that he has been sleepwalking through life.

> How I got into it I cannot clearly say
> for I was moving like a sleepwalker
> the moment I stepped out of the right way.[1]

Sleepwalking through life is a spiritual insanity that imperceptibly accumulates over the years into a vague faceless fear or regret of something that we cannot name. We become haunted by a ghost, the unlived portion of our lives.

Toward the end of his life, Henry James wrote a haunting autobiographical story entitled "The Jolly Corner" in which Spencer Brydon encounters the unlived portion of his life. At age fifty-six, Spencer returns from Europe to his native New York, after an absence of thirty-three years. In his old family home Spencer encounters a ghost, a disfigured alter ego, the person he might have been had he never gone abroad.

James wrote this story when he was sixty-two upon returning to his native New York after an absence of twenty-nine years. At this time he was reviewing old notebooks where he reencountered inspirations for stories that he had never taken time to develop. "The Jolly Corner" reflects something that haunted James most of his life—neglected opportunities.[2] "Footfalls echo in the memory down the passage we did not take towards the door we never opened...."[3]

Like James, our memory takes us back to old haunts that we have not visited for years. In these journeys, all the "what might have beens," the "what ifs," and "if onlys" of a lifetime echo in our minds. There, all our vacant, unattended moments and roads not taken distill into one doleful word, *regret*. As we approach death and begin to see things in the light of eternity, our regrets begin to undergo a metamorphosis.

The regrets of missed business opportunities begin to pale in comparison with missed opportunities to spend time with one's spouse, children, or friends. The regret of not being more successful in our chosen career gives way to the piercing knowledge that we have ignored or not attended to a deeper vision, a deeper calling for our lives that we have intuited since childhood.

Shortly before her death, Claire Booth Luce, one of the most successful American women—congresswoman, ambassador, playwright—said, "If I were to write an autobiography, my title would be *The Autobiography of a Failure*." Her explanation for this astounding verdict passed upon her own life was that she had listened to an "outer voice" (that of her husband Henry Luce, who prodded her to run for Congress) instead of heeding her "inner voice" to follow her real vocation in life. "My failure was not to return to the real vocation I had, which was writing."[4]

The soul's deepest regret is that it hasn't heeded its true vocation, the call to love. It is the rending regret of our deepest intimations of what we are called to be as creatures made in the image and likeness of God. But this regret is unattended. It is so buried under such a mound of preoccupations that, often, we experience it only indirectly in projection.

Why do we envy Scrooge at the end of Dickens's story *A Christmas Carol* if not for the reason that something deep inside of us recognizes our true self that yearns to be like Scrooge, a person who has come home to himself, has discovered at last that true joy only resides in a loving heart that reflects its creator, and rejoices in the knowledge that "this is the reason I was born"?

An often overlooked but significant detail of Dickens's story is that it ends exactly where it began, in Scrooge's counting-house. Scrooge's transformation did not whisk him away to a monastery or take him to the foreign missions. It led him back to his place of employment, and there he discovered something wonderful that he had been blind to for years: Bob Cratchit was a fellow human being. Scrooge arrived where he had started and knew the place for the first time.

The same is true for us. The grace of transformation may, at times, beckon us to walk down paths unknown, but more often than not, grace leads us back to our daily rounds. And there, like Scrooge, we encounter the same people we have lived and worked with for years.

The circumstances of Thérèse's life, like our own, were ordinary. Every day she awoke to deal with the same people and same situations that she had dealt with the day before. However, her life was not boring because she consciously attended to the greatest adventure of all,

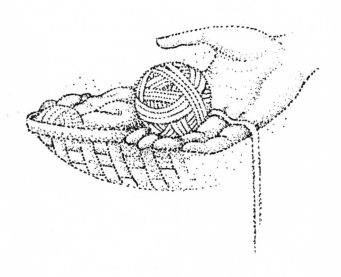

"penetrating into the mysterious depths of charity."[5] Thérèse's "little way" discloses to us the inexhaustible depths of the commonplace, where each choice to love is that point of intersection of the timeless with time, where the impossible union, the mystery of the Incarnation, takes place in our lives. Love is a step-by-step journey into the heartland of the ordinary, choice upon choice, choice within choice. Thérèse wrote:

> One day, Léonie, thinking she was too big to be playing any longer with dolls, came to us with a basket filled with dresses and pretty pieces for making others; her doll was resting on top. "Here, my little sisters, *choose*; I'm giving you all this." Céline stretched out her hand and took a little ball of wool which pleased her. After a moment's reflection I stretched out mine saying: "I choose all!" and I took the basket without further ceremony.... This little incident of my childhood is a summary of my whole life; later on when perfection was set before me, I understood that to become a *saint* one had to suffer much, seek out always the most perfect thing to do, and forget self. I understood, too, that there are many degrees of perfection and each soul was free to respond to the advances of Our Lord, to do little or much for Him, in a word, to *choose* among the sacrifices He was asking. Then as in the days of my childhood, I cried out: "My God '*I choose all!*' I don't want to be a *saint by halfs*, I'm not afraid to suffer for You, I fear only one thing: to keep my *own will*; so take it, for '*I choose all*' that You will!"[6]

This is also a metaphor of our own lives. Each day the drama of choice confronts us. We are free to respond to or avoid the opportunities to love that God sets before us.

To love is a fearful thing because it threatens to change our lives, to rob us of what we cling to: time, energy, and the like. However, by not loving, we deprive ourselves of what we need, God's life. How many times a day do we cheat ourselves out of an act of love or in guarded circumspection measure out our response in coffee spoons?

But what we measure out is measured back to us, and what we withhold from others, we withhold from ourselves. "To cheat oneself out of love is the most terrible deception," writes Kierkegaard; "It is an eternal loss for which there is no reparation, either in time or eternity."[7] This is why Thérèse did not want to be a saint by halves. She did not want to be cheated out of life. She wanted to be whole, to be sane.

In the introduction to this book I said that I would not be writing about the spirituality of St. Thérèse as a way to holiness but as a means to sanity. However, as I drew nearer to the conclusion of this book I realized that I could not separate the two. For to be deeply sane is to be deeply holy.

Thérèse stayed sane because she stayed rooted in God's life. It was the taproot and wellspring of all her actions. "Never have I heard Him speak, but I feel He is within me, at each moment...guiding and inspiring me with what to say and do...."[8]

When we fail to live in God's presence, we no longer see things *sub specie aeternitatis*, which sheds meaning on all the disparate parts of our lives and unifies the whole. We feel fragmented. Our lives seem like a random series of disconnected events or a pocket full of odds and ends. What we need to recover, writes James Hillman, is "a sense of personal calling, that there is a reason why I am alive."[9]

Shortly before Thérèse died she wondered what her specific calling in the church was. Her deep desire to love God with the love of Jesus made her vocation as a Carmelite feel constricting. She wrote:

> To be your *Spouse*, to be a *Carmelite*, and by my union with You to be the *Mother* of souls, should not this suffice me? And yet it is not so. No doubt, these three privileges sum up my true *vocation*: *Carmelite*, *Spouse*, *Mother*, and yet I feel within me other vocations. I feel the vocation of the WARRIOR, THE PRIEST, THE APOSTLE, THE DOCTOR, THE MARTYR. Finally, I feel the need and the desire of carrying out the most heroic deeds for *You, O Jesus*.[10]

The solution of how her immense desire to love would be actualized was revealed to her as she read St. Paul's famous chapter on love in 1 Corinthians. There she discovered that love is the universal ground and eternal form that undergirds and unifies all vocations.

> I finally had rest. Considering the mystical body of the Church, I had not recognized myself in any of the members described by St. Paul, or rather I desired to see myself in them *all*. *Charity* gave me the key to my *vocation*. I understood that if the

Church had a body composed of different members, the most necessary and most noble of all could not be lacking to it, and so I understood that the Church *has a Heart and that this Heart was* BURNING WITH LOVE. *I understood it was Love alone* that made the Church's members act, that if Love ever became extinct, apostles would not preach the Gospel and martyrs would not shed their blood. I understood that LOVE COMPRISED ALL VOCATIONS, THAT LOVE WAS EVERYTHING, THAT IT EMBRACED ALL TIMES AND PLACES...IN A WORD, THAT IT WAS ETERNAL!

Then, in the excess of my delirious joy, I cried out: O Jesus, my love...my *vocation*, at last I have found it...MY VOCATION IS LOVE!

Yes, I have found my place in the Church.... I shall be *Love.* Thus I shall be everything and thus my dream will be realized.[11]

I have found my place. This is where I belong. Thérèse was home at last because she was at home with herself and with God. Thérèse was given a peace beyond understanding because it quelled all of her nagging doubts about the adequacy of her life.

Before Thérèse was given the grace of knowing that her vocation was love, she had unconscious misgivings about her relationship to God. Was she truly pleasing to God? Were her trivial actions enough in God's sight? Was she required to perform some daring feat of glory?

These questions manifested themselves in a dream she had had several months before. In the dream she asked Blessed Anne of Jesus: "Mother, tell me further if God is not asking something more of me than my poor little actions and desires. Is He content with me?" Blessed Anne answered, "He is content, very content!"[12]

When Thérèse awoke she felt a deep peace, but it was only months later that this grace flowered into consciousness. It was only when she discovered that her vocation was love that she could say, "I finally had rest.... I have found my place." Thérèse was finally at home with herself, for she was given the assurance that what she was doing was enough in the sight of God.

To be at home with ourselves, we too need to quell the nagging doubt about the adequacy of our lives before God. We need to believe that God is content with us.

"Consider your life," writes Jean-Pierre de Caussade, "and you will see that it consists of countless trifling actions. Yet God is quite satisfied with them, for doing them as they should be done is the part we have to play in our striving for perfection."[13] And perfection is not beyond our grasp.

"Perfection consists in doing His will, in being what He wills us to be," writes Thérèse.[14] God does not expect us to be something that we are not. God asks only one thing of us and that is for us to love. And love is not beyond our grasp.

> I have no other means of proving my love for you [my God] than that of strewing flowers, that is, not allowing one little sacrifice to escape, not one look, one word, profiting by all the smallest things and doing them through love.[15]

This is not a sentimentalizing of the minuscule, but an expression of an authentic life, the true occupation of the saint. For we can only love, says William Blake, in "minute particulars." Love is always concrete, never abstract, never a vague mood, always a tangible choice.

Consider your life for a moment. What does it consist of except minute particulars? What else do you have to prove your love except a thought, a word, a look, a deed? That is all that any of us have; yet God is satisfied with our tokens of love.

It is the love of God dwelling in our actions that makes us whole. It is love that keeps us sane.

Notes

Introduction

    1. Guy Gaucher, *The Story of a Life: St. Thérèse of Lisieux*, trans. Anne Marie Brennan (San Francisco: Harper & Row, 1987), p. 2.

    2. Barry Ulanov, *The Making of a Saint: A Biographical Study of Thérèse of Lisieux* (Garden City, N.Y.: Doubleday, 1966), p. v.

    3. Christopher O'Mahony, ed. and trans. *St. Thérèse of Lisieux: By Those Who Knew Her* (Dublin: Veritas Publications, 1975), p. 51.

    4. St. Thérèse of Lisieux, *Story of a Soul*, trans. John Clarke, O.C.D. (Washington, D.C.: ICS Publications, 1976), p. 222.

    5. Thérèse, *Story of a Soul*, p. 223.

    6. O'Mahony, p. 49.

    7. O'Mahony, p. 119.

    8. O'Mahony, p. 120.

Chapter One. The Secrets That Keep Us Sane

Epigraph: Emily Dickinson, poem 303, "The Soul selects her own Society," in *The Complete Poems of Emily Dickinson* (Boston: Little, Brown, 1960), p. 143.

1. Sissela Bok, *Secrets* (New York: Vintage Books, 1989), pp. 5–6.

2. Carl Jung, *Modern Man in Search of a Soul*, trans. W. S. Dell and Carey F. Baynes (New York: Harcourt, 1933), p. 35.

3. Carl Jung, *Memories, Dreams, Reflections*, recorded and edited by Aniela Jaffe, trans. Richard and Clara Winston (London: Random House, 1963), pp. 143–45.

4. Robert Frost, "The Secret Sits," in *The Poetry of Robert Frost* (New York: Holt, Rinehart and Winston, 1967), p. 362.

5. Charles Dickens, "The Holly-Tree," in *Christmas Stories* (Oxford: Oxford University Press, 1987), p. 107.

6. Thérèse, *Story of a Soul*, p. 66.

7. Thérèse, *Story of a Soul*, pp. 66–67.

8. St. John of the Cross, "The Living Flame of Love," in *The Collected Works of St. John of the Cross*, trans. Kieran Kavanaugh, O.C.D. and Otilio Rodriguez, O.C.D. (Washington, D.C.: ICS Publications, 1991), stanza 3, par. 34, p. 687.

9. Thérèse, *Story of a Soul*, p. 77.

10. Marie-Louise von Franz, "The Process of Individuation," in *Man and His Symbols*, ed. Carl Jung (New York: Dell Publishing, 1964), p. 209.

11. Russell Lockhart, *Words as Eggs*, quoted from Helen Luke, *Kaleidoscope: The Way of Women and Other Essays*, ed. Rob Baker (New York: Parabola Books, 1992), p. 119.

12. Stephen King, "The Body," in *Different Seasons* (New York: The Penguin Group, 1982), p. 390.

13. Thérèse, *Story of a Soul*, p. 125.

14. St. John of the Cross, *The Ascent of Mount Carmel*, bk. 3, chap. 13, par. 6, p. 288.

15. Karen Horney, *Neurosis and Human Growth* (New York: W. W. Norton, 1950), p. 18.

Chapter Two. Finding Her Way

Epigraph: St. Thérèse of Lisieux, "My Heaven on Earth," in *The Poetry of St. Thérèse of Lisieux*, trans. Donald Kinney, O.C.D. (Washington, D.C.: ICS Publications, 1995, p. 109.

1. Ida Gorres, *The Hidden Face: A Study of St. Thérèse of Lisieux*, trans. Richard and Clara Winston (New York: Pantheon Books, 1959), p. 305.

2. André Combes, *St. Thérèse and Her Mission*, trans. Alastair Guinan (New York: P. J. Kennedy & Sons, 1955), pp. 134–35.

3. Gaucher, p. 88.

4. St. Thérèse of Lisieux, *Her Last Conversations*, trans. John Clarke, O.C.D. (Washington, D.C.: ICS Publications, 1977), p. 115.

5. Thérèse, *Story of a Soul*, p. 169.

6. Thérèse, *Story of a Soul*, p. 169.

7. Thérèse, *Story of a Soul*, pp. 169–70.

8. Thérèse, *Last Conversations*, p. 77.

9. Patricia O'Connor, *In Search of St. Thérèse* (Collegeville, Minn.: Liturgical Press, 1987), p. 62.

10. Thérèse, *Last Conversations*, p. 130.

11. Thérèse, *Story of a Soul*, p. 87.

12. See Canto 23 of Dante's *Inferno*.

13. O'Mahony, p. 197.

14. O'Mahony, p. 196.

15. St. Thérèse of Lisieux, *General Correspondence*, vol. 1, trans. John Clarke, O.C.D. (Washington, D.C.: ICS Publications, 1982), p. 427.

16. Conrad De Meester, *With Empty Hands*, trans. Anne Marie, O.C.D. (Homebush, New South Wales: St. Paul Publications, 1982), p. 26.

17. Dorothy Donnelly, "Smiled At," in *The Palace of Being: New and Selected Poems* (Chicago: Loyola University Press, 1990), p. 16.

18. I am indebted to Ernest S. Wolf for the idea behind this mental exercise. See his book *Treating the Self: Elements in Clinical Self Psychology* (New York: Guilford Press, 1988), pp. 26–27.

19. For a good treatment of Freud's concept of the Über-Ich, see Bruno Bettelheim, *Freud and Man's Soul* (New York: Vintage Books, 1984), pp. 57–59; and Theodor Reik, *Listening with the Third Ear: The Inner Experience of a Psychoanalyst* (New York: Pyramid Books, 1948), pp. 15–18.

20. Hans Christian Andersen, "The Ugly Duckling," in *The Complete Fairy Tales and Stories*, trans. Erik Christian Haugaard (Garden City, N.Y.: Anchor Press/ Doubleday, 1983), p. 219.

21. Andersen, p. 222.

22. Dante Alighieri, *The Divine Comedy*, *Vol. 3: Paradise*, trans. Dorothy L. Sayers and Barbara Reynolds (Baltimore: Penguin Books, 1962), Canto 29, p. 309.

23. Dante Alighieri, *The Divine Comedy*, *Vol. 1: Inferno*, trans. Mark Musa (New York: Penguin Books, 1971), Canto 23, p. 279.

Chapter Three. The Sanity of Silence

Epigraph: St. John of the Cross, "The Saying of Light and Love," in *The Collected Works of St. John of the Cross*, p. 92.

1. Max Picard, *The World of Silence*, trans. Stanley Godman (Chicago: Henry Regnery Company, 1952), p. 45.

2. Thérèse, *Story of a Soul*, p. 179.

3. Bernard Bro, *The Little Way*, trans. Alan Neamne (Westminster, Md.: Christian Classics, 1980), p. 34.

4. Bro, p. 34.

5. Thérèse, *Last Conversations*, p. 38.

6. O'Mahony, p. 31.

7. Thérèse, *Last Conversations*, p. 39.

8. Thérèse, *Story of a Soul*, p. 239.

9. O'Mahony, p. 120.

10. Rainer Maria Rilke, "The Man Watching," in *The Rag and Bone Shop of the Heart: Poems for Men*, trans. Robert Bly, ed. Robert Bly, James Hillman, Michael Meade (New York: HarperCollins, 1992), p. 298.

11. Thérèse, *Story of a Soul*, p. 223.

12. Thérèse, *Story of a Soul*, p. 224.

13. Thérèse, *Story of a Soul*, p. 224.

14. Thérèse, *Story of a Soul*, p. 224.

15. Geneviève of the Holy Face (Céline Martin), *A Memoir of my sister St. Thérèse*, trans. Carmelite Sisters of New York (New York: P. J. Kenedy & Sons, 1959), p. 31.

16. Thérèse, *Last Conversations*, p. 36.

17. O'Mahony, p. 51.

18. Geneviève, p. 61.

19. Thérèse, *Last Conversations*, p. 138.

20. Thérèse, *Last Conversations*, p. 16.

21. Carol Tarvis, *Anger, The Misunderstood Emotion* (New York: Simon & Schuster, 1982), pp. 143–44.

22. St. John of the Cross, "Counsels to a Religious on How to Reach Perfection," in *The Collected Works of St. John of the Cross*, pp. 725–26.

23. St. Bernard of Clairvaux, "On the Steps of Pride and Humility," in *Bernard of Clairvaux: Selected Works*, trans. G. R. Evans (New York: Paulist Press, 1987), p. 123.

24. O'Mahony, p. 144.

25. O'Mahony, p. 121.

26. David Shapiro, *Neurotic Styles* (New York: Basic Books, 1965), p. 136.

27. Thérèse, *Story of a Soul*, p. 252.

28. Geneviève, p. 99.

29. Geneviève, p. 99.

30. St. Teresa of Avila, "The Interior Castle," in *The Collected Works of St. Teresa of Avila*, vol. 2, trans. Otilio Rodriguez, O.C.D. and Kieran Kavanaugh, O.C.D. (Washington, D.C.: ICS Publications, 1980), p. 449.

31. Robert Johnson, *Transformations* (San Francisco: HarperCollins, 1991), p. 6.

32. Dorothy L. Sayers, *Introductory Papers on Dante* (New York: Harper and Brothers, 1953), p. 61.

33. Geneviève, p. 67.

34. Geneviève, p. 67.

35. St. John of the Cross, "The Dark Night of the Soul," in *The Collected Works of St. John of the* Cross, bk. 1, chap. 14, p. 393.

Chapter Four. The Sanity of Loving Freely

Epigraph: T. S. Eliot, "East Coker," in *Four Quartets* (New York: Harcourt, 1971), p. 31.

1. The author has made every possible effort to find the exact location of this quote, but to no avail.

2. Thérèse, *Last Conversations*, p. 44.

3. Geneviève, pp. 5–6.

4. T. S. Eliot, "Ash-Wednesday," in *T. S. Eliot: Selected Poems* (New York: Harcourt, 1964), p. 93.

5. Thérèse, *Last Conversations*, p. 42.

6. Pierre Descouvement, *Thérèse and Lisieux*, trans. Salvatore Sciurba, O.C.D. and Louise Pambrum (Grand Rapids: Wm. B. Eerdmans, 1996), p. 203.

7. Thérèse, *Story of a Soul*, p. 222.

Chapter Five. The Divine Perspective of Charity

Epigraph: William Wordsworth, "Lines Written a few miles above Tintern Abbey," in *William Wordsworth*, ed. Stephen Gill (Oxford: Oxford University Press, 1984), pp. 132–33.

1. Thomas Merton, *The Sign of Jonas: The Journal of Thomas Merton* (New York: Harcourt, 1953), pp. 91–92.

2. Geneviève, p. 76.

3. St. John of the Cross, "The Living Flame of Love," in *The Collected Works of St. John of the Cross*, stanza 4, par. 5, p. 710.

4. St. Teresa of Avila, "The Way of Perfection," in *The Collected Works of St. Teresa of Avila*, vol. 2, p. 64.

5. Frederick Faber, "Kindness," in *Spiritual Conferences* (Philadelphia: Peter Reilly Co., 1957), pp. 27–28.

6. Jon Hassler, *North of Hope* (New York: Ballantine Books, 1990), pp. 173–74.

7. Thérèse, *Story of a Soul*, pp. 247–48.

8. Thérèse, *Story of a Soul*, p. 248.

9. St. John of the Cross, "The Dark Night of the Soul," in *The Collected Works of St. John of the Cross*, bk.2, chap. 4, p. 400.

10. Geneviève, p. 28.

11. O'Mahony, p. 94.

12. Thérèse, *Story of a Soul*, pp. 219–20.

13. O'Mahony, pp. 50–51.

14. Thérèse, *Story of a Soul*, p. 179.

Chapter Six. An Attended Life, an Authentic Life

Epigraph: T. S. Eliot, "The Dry Salvages," in *Four Quartets* (New York: Harcourt, 1971), p. 44.

1. Dante Alighieri, *Inferno: Translation by Twenty Contemporary Poets*, ed. Daniel Malpern, Canto 1, trans. Seamus Heaney (Hopewell, N.J.: Ecco Press, 1993), p. 3.

2. Millicent Bell, *Meaning in Henry James* (Cambridge, Mass.: Harvard University Press, 1991). See chap. 11, "The Presence of Potentiality: 'The Jolly Corner.'"

3. T. S. Eliot, "Burnt Norton," in *Four Quartets* (New York: Harcourt, 1971), p. 13.

4. Carole Klein and Richard Gotti, *Overcoming Regret* (New York: Bantam Books, 1992), p. 46.

5. Thérèse, *Story of a Soul*, p. 233.

6. Thérèse, *Story of a Soul*, p. 27.

7. Søren Kierkegaard, *Works of Love: Some Christian Reflections in the Form of Discourses*, trans. Howard and Edna Hung, New York: Harper & Row, 1962), p. 23.

8. Thérèse, *Story of a Soul*, p. 179.

9. James Hillman, *The Soul's Code: In Search of Character and Calling* (New York: Random House, 1996), p. 4.

10. Thérèse, *Story of a Soul*, p. 192.

11. Thérèse, *Story of a Soul*, p. 194.

12. Thérèse, *Story of a Soul*, p. 191.

13. Jean-Pierre De Caussade, *Abandonment to Divine Providence* (Garden City, N.Y.: Image Books, 1966), p. 25.

14. Thérèse, *Story of a Soul*, p. 14.

15. Thérèse, *Story of a Soul*, p. 196.

ILLUMINATIONBOOKS

Other Books in the Series

Little Pieces of Light...Darkness and Personal Growth
    by Joyce Rupp

Lessons from the Monastery That Touch Your Life
    by M. Basil Pennington, O.C.S.O.

As You and the Abused Person Journey Together
    by Sharon E. Cheston

Spirituality, Stress & You
    by Thomas E. Rodgerson

Joy, The Dancing Spirit of Love Surrounding You
    by Beverly Elaine Eanes

Every Decision You Make Is a Spiritual One
    by Anthony J. De Conciliis with John F. Kinsella

Celebrating the Woman You Are
    by S. Suzanne Mayer, I.H.M.

Why Are You Worrying?
    by Joseph W. Ciarrocchi

Partners in the Divine Dance of Our Three Person'd God
    by Shaun McCarty, S.T.

Love God...Clean House...Help Others
    by Duane F. Reinert, O.F.M. Cap.

Along Your Desert Journey
    by Robert M. Hamma

Appreciating God's Creation Through Scripture
    by Alice L. Laffey

Let Yourself Be Loved
    by Phillip Bennett

Facing Discouragement
    by Kathleen Fischer and Thomas Hart

Living Simply in an Anxious World
    by Robert J. Wicks

A Rainy Afternoon with God
    by Catherine B. Cawley

Time, A Collection of Fragile Moments
    by Joan Monahan

15 Ways to Nourish Your Faith
    by Susan Shannon Davies

Following in the Footsteps of Jesus
    by Gerald D. Coleman, S.S. and David M. Pettingill

God Lives Next Door
    by Lyle K. Weiss

Hear the Just Word & Live It
    by Walter J. Burghardt, S.J.